Tennessee Williams

A Portrait in Laughter and Lamentation

Tennessee Williams

A Portrait in Laughter and Lamentation

Harry Rasky

Mosaic Press
OAKVILLE, ON — NIAGARA FALLS, NY

Grateful acknowledgement is made to the following for permission to use quotations:
Arthur Miller, Jack Miller, Rex Reed. *Los Angeles Times* (Cecil Smith and Dan Sullivan
film reviews). *The Miami Herald* (interview). *New York Post* (Earl Wilson column). 1.
Quote from Brooks Atkinson (Tennessee Williams). 2. Quote from Clive Barnes, of April
3, 1972 ("Small Craft Warnings"). 3. "Depending on the Kindness of Public TV, "by John
O'Connor, of December 8 1976. 4. Quote from John Leonard, of June 13, 1976. Copyright © 1972/76 by The New York Times Company. Reprinted by permission. *TIME:*
Excerpts from "Clinging to a Spar." "The Angel of the Odd." "The Crack-Up." Copyright
19-Time Inc. All rights reserved. Reprinted by permission from TIME.

Cover Design by Amy V. Land

Published by MOSAIC PRESS, P.O. Box 1032, Oakville, Ontario, L6J 5E9, Canada. Offices
and warehouse at 1252 Speers Road, Units #1&2, Oakville, Ontario, L6L 5N9, Canada and
Mosaic Press, 4500 Witmer Industrial Estates, PMB 145, Niagara Falls, NY 14305-1386

Mosaic Press acknowledges the assistance of the Canada Council, the Ontario Arts Council
and the Department of Canadian Heritage, Government of Canada for their support of our
publishing programme.

MOSAIC PRESS, in Canada:
1252 Speers Road, Units #1 & 2,
Oakville, Ontario, L6L 5N9
Phone / Fax: 905-825-2130
mosaicpress@aibn.on.ca

The Canada Council Le Conseil des Arts
FOR THE ARTS   DU CANADA
SINCE 1957   DEPUIS 1957

MOSAIC PRESS, in the USA:
4500 Witmer Industrial Estates
PMB 145, Niagara Falls, NY
14305-1386 Tel:1-800-387-8992
mosaicpress@aibn.on.ca

For Ruth Arlene,
whom Tennessee always said he had invented

FILMS BY HARRY RASKY

William Hutt: A Most Fortunate Man, 1997
Christopher Plummer: King of Players, 1995
The War Against the Indians, 1992
The Magic Season of Robertson Davies, 1990
The Great Teacher: Northrop Frye, 1989
Degas, 1987-88
To Mend the world, 1986
Karsh: The Searching Eye, 1985-86
The Mystery of Henry Moore, 1985
Raymond Massey: Actor of The Century, 1984
Stratasphere, 1983
The Spies Who Never Were, 1981
Being Different- feature, 1981
The Man Who Hid Anne Frank, 1981
The Song of Leonard Cohen, 1981
Arthur Miller On Home Ground, 1979
The Lessons of History, Will and Ariel Durant, 1978
The Peking Man Mystery, 1977
Homage to Chagall, 1976-77
Travels Through Life With Leacock, 1975
Next Year In Jerusalem, 1974
Baryshnikov, 1974
Tennessee Williams' South, 1973
The Wit and World of G. Bernard Shaw, 1972
Upon This Rock, 1972
Hall of Kings, 1967
Operation Sea War - Vietnam
A Tour of Washington with Mrs. Lyndon Johnson
The Nobel Prize Awards
The Twentieth Century
NBC White Paper - Panama; Danger Zone
Cuba and Castro Today

Videocassettes of Harry Rasky's documentary,
*Tennessee Williams: A Portrait in Laughter and
Lamentation*, are available from Mosaic Press.

Every genuine work of art has as much reason for being as the earth and the sun. There is properly no history, only biography.
– Emerson

TO TENNESSEE IN THE YEAR 2000

As I sit writing this to you, on my balcony overlooking the still waters of the Gulf of Mexico in Sarasota, I feel somewhat lost in what you called "the Perhaps".... So much has happened since we first met thirty years ago in New York and you agreed to join me in creating our film *Tennessee Williams' South*.

I remember how you suffered so with your eyes. The irony is that Adam, our son who looked so asthmatic and frail then, is now a robust, muscular, brilliant eye surgeon. You would love him as much as he adores your work. You may recall you wrote in my daughter's autograph book "for Holly Laura many laurels." She is now a sensitive woman and an attorney.

Yes, "baby" as you would say, we have crossed over that great divide into a new nervous millennium. All those zeroes!!

Your poetry and plays made us all so much more human. Your works are more popular now than ever, anywhere, even though you told me you didn't care if you were remembered after your death. Liberty has been taken with your wishes and works. They carried you back to St. Louis in a coffin – the city from which you escaped. And your beloved sister Rose is finally gone. The sad suffering gone.

The Redgraves resurrected your earliest play and it was wildly praised on Broadway as one of the most important events of the year. They turned *Streetcar Named Desire* into an opera of indefinite quality even though you said many times while we were together for those madly memorable lunches at the Monkey Bar at the Elysee Hotel that you opposed the concept of adding music to that classic. "Baby, leave it be." Your poetry has its own music. And guess what? The best foreign film of the year, *All About my Mother* is by a Spanish director Almodovar, a mother-haunted man, as you were, and it has its central theme the poetry and pain of *Streetcar*. Not everyone is "hanging back with the brutes". I could hear your deep-from-the-soul lament that was your laugh filling Gulf of Mexico Drive. "What will they think of next baby," you might have said.

Oh, Tennessee, I think so often daily as I listen to the gentle waves, what we all have learned from you. You wrote in *Night of the Iguana*, part of which I staged so long ago in our film: "You know how much we need still water."

I am now near the age you were when you left us. I understand so much about fear. In *Outcry* you cried out about "Fear – the fearless little man with the drum inside the rib-cage – fear grown to panic."

Perhaps I dwell too much in the shelter of our friendship. Perhaps...Perhaps...But I do have a unique view you were so kind to allow.

Elia Kazan once told me he was astonished at how faithful I remain to you.

I am pleased our time together is coming out in this new edition.

Forgive me, friend, if I paraphrase your great, eloquent soliloquy that is at the end of *The Glass Menagerie*:

I attempted to find in motion what was lost in space.

I traveled around a great deal. The cities swept about me like dead leaves, leaves that were brightly colored but torn away from the branches.

I would have stopped, but I was pursued by something.

It always came upon me unawares, taking me altogether by surprise. Perhaps it was a familiar bit of music. Perhaps it was only a piece of transparent glass –

Perhaps I am walking along a street at night, in some strange city, before I found companions.

I pass the lighted window of a shop where perfume is sold.

The window is filled with pieces of colored glass, tiny transparent bottles in delicate colors like bits of a shattered rainbow.

Then, all at once you touch my shoulder. I turn around and look into your eyes.

Oh, Tennessee, Tennessee, I tried to leave you behind me, but I am more faithful then I intended to be!

I reach for a cigar, I cross the street. I run into the movies or a bar. I buy a drink. I speak to the nearest stranger – anything that can blow your candles out!

For nowadays the world is lit by lighting! Blow out your candles, Tennessee –and so good-bye...

Perhaps

Love,
Harry Rasky
Sarasota, 2000

Now I see the sorrow. But what I hear is the laughter. Tennessee said that laughing was his way of lamenting. I know now how much he wept for us all.

O N MY OFFICE WALL, facing the winter sun, are three faded photographs that speak softly of his frailty. The pink and gold are gone; the colors will not hold. The February glare has bleached out all but the ghostly white on white and has shaded the blue into an abstract gray. Wisdom requires that the prints be moved, stored in some impersonal file or dark drawer for safekeeping. But somehow, I cannot hide them in some impersonal hideaway.

In one photo, he sits studying a slim volume of poems at our café in New Orleans. The film "clapboard" beside him reminds me of the cameras on the roadside. And the tape recorder that would pick up "wild track"—he loved that phrase, *wild track*, a term for unsynchronized sound. In the second print, he sits on the edge of a fishing boat, off the coast of Key West, now paled by snow reflected from Bay Street behind the photo. He stares into the now-silent sea where he told me he wished to be buried beside the fragments of Hart Crane, a poet-comrade of an earlier time. His wish was denied in death; he is resting I think so uncomfortably beside his overpowering mother, Edwina, in the St. Louis that pained him so in life. No rest for him even in death. The third photo is of the rectory in Columbus, Mississippi, where he was born those seventy-odd years ago. Like a transparent curtain, it seems to have vanished almost into a subtle southern wind.

Lamentations?

No, not quite. Because the sound of that laughter—a cackle almost—the life force that was Tennessee, obeys no rules. Before my memory of him fades further, like those snapshot seconds on the wall, I feel obliged to share him with you. And it is the laughter, now filling my head, now filling screens and theaters, painful, joyous laughter, that haunts my memory of Tennessee Williams' South.

> I think we are all winners and losers in rotation, you know. We go through periods of winning and through periods of losing. Losing is a hard habit to break.

To begin.

It's been more than a decade and a half since he came into my life. There were meetings at lunch at the Monkey Bar in New York (how many stuffed peppers can you eat?); filming sessions in Key West, New Orleans, and New York—the supposed purpose of it all, cinema in New York and theater in Hollywood, the opposite of the usual because there was never anything usual with Tennessee; a collaboration in Atlanta (he the writer, I the director); and dinners in London and even Toronto. Phone calls, letters, shared laughter. A few terrible opening nights (oh, the pain). We became, what? Friends? More than that: "soul brothers," he liked to say. Our meeting now seemed more fated than accidental, more predetermined than casual. And frankly, I came to love him.

It was a time of his suffering. I never knew him before that "rotation" from winner to loser in the public eye. In my eye, he was never that.

He was brought to me, like most of the important and meaningful events in my life, by my wife, Arlene. She has always known how to push my imagination beyond the imaginable. I was finishing my first film for the Canadian Broadcasting Corporation in Toronto. The title was *The Wit and World of G. Bernard Shaw*. It had gone well. I had been able to explore the Dublin haunts of Shaw's lonely childhood, the bravado of his writings, the delicious humor of his stage preachings in London. I came to know much about his locale and his eloquent keening about his Irish brothers. I still smile at his epigrams ("A lifetime of happiness—it would be hell on earth"). But I never knew him. I especially did not know, could not know, how he felt about sex, about women. I know what he wrote. But like most great writers, he constantly contradicted himself in print. All through my year with him, the time of working on the film, I

2

wanted to say, "Will the real Bernard Shaw stand now? And tell the truth, the real truth!" That never happened, and now we'll never know. I've wondered often since then how many questions would now be answered if there had been film and the way I have come to use it when Shakespeare lived. What did he really have in mind when he wrote "To be or not to be," and why is "This above all, to thine own self be true" always played for laughs? Surely no laughing matter.

Tennessee was brought to me in 1971 in the form of an article by Rex Reed that had been currently appearing in *Esquire* magazine. We were visiting our New York apartment at 11 Waverly Place, Penthouse B, dusting a month or so of New York off our furniture, and I was exploring our future. The seventies were under way. I had taken refuge in my native Canada while America was being mugged by history: assassinations of ideas and men, the dual obscenities of Vietnam and Watergate. I needed a subject, and Arlene, herself a gentle and complex product of the South, urged—no, insisted—that I read the piece on Tennessee.

I thought it had a kind of catty brutality about it. It was called "Tennessee Williams Turns Sixty" and was subheaded with a nasty "Nobody, absolutely *nobody*, knows the troubles he's seen." There were some eight pages of clawing that began:

> "Baby, I've been sick." Tennessee Williams sits under a chandelier sporting a rosy suntan and a freshly thatched beard, having dinner at Antoine's. . . . If a swamp alligator could talk, he would sound like Tennessee Williams. His tongue seems coated with rum and molasses as it darts in and out of his mouth, licking at his moustache like a pink lizard. . . . At the age of sixty the world's most famous playwright stands precariously on the ledge of vulnerability, fighting like a jaguar and talking like a poet. "The carrion birds have tried to peck out my eyes and my tongue and my mind, but they've never been able to get at my heart."

What kind of world and man would this be? How distant from the relatively square sanctuary of my existence! But I had claimed that I wanted to dig deeper, feel what others really felt and to somehow marry that to film. There was a paragraph of intense

3

sensibility among the flora and fauna of Rex Reed prose. I could not turn away from it.

> Years of indescribable torment and physical dissipation that taught him a way of life. Even now, he still wanders restlessly in search of the sad music in people, ordering a banquet for the spirit, and although he has always got what he asked for, the melody has often been in the wrong key and the meal served at inconvenient hours. And out of the loneliness and self-destruction and pain have come some of the world's greatest plays. Why do they survive along with him? Why does Tennessee Williams, already written off by the cynics in the obituaries they keep taking out and rattling whenever a new play opens, make more comebacks than Judy Garland? Because in an age so filled with non-appreciation and polite sensibility, a time of fatalism, nihilism, a certain destruction of the ideal of beauty, a replacement by wastelands and other sterile sanctuaries, he suffers the urgent need to bring meaning to life, to resurrect gentility and kindness. It is not necessary to understand him to appreciate his genius. One needs only to feel and he *feels* magnificently.

Amen! I say now. But then, but then, I was not yet searching deep enough. Deep into where the lamentations and laughter became the same human outcry.

There was a closing quote that bathed the man in a kind of humor that had instant appeal. Tennessee said, "I told my friend Gore Vidal, I said, 'Gore, baby, I slept through the Sixties,' and my friend Gore, he said, 'You didn't miss a thing!'"

So I would try. I would try to make Tennessee a subject. After all, how could it affect me? Studying a man for a film would be like cramming for an exam: Once the date is spewed out, who remembers? How many chemistry formulae and Latin names for bugs have we all forgotten?

I knew a little about him but little realized how much that had already dug into my being. As a student at the University of Toronto, long before jets shamed time, I had driven a day and a night to spend a week in New York. My brother Frank, then a *Variety* reviewer, had arranged for tickets to see the hits of the day, and 1948 was, as they say, a very good vintage year. Sitting on the steps in the second balcony of a sellout house, I was a witness to *A Streetcar Named Desire* when it was still blessed with Tandy and Brando. It was a revelation, like a dark rainbow of amber and indigo and many shades of purple. The poetry and music molded a kind of magic in my twenty-year-old Canadian mind, even then. And when an usher sat down to join us, I asked, "They're laughing. Why are they laughing? Isn't it a tragedy?" She said, "They always laugh. Too close for comfort, I suppose. But they leave weeping." And I can recall walking down Broadway, my first night on Broadway, wanting to wash the images from my mind. The neon pavement seemed to be a huge reflection of the set I had just left. And the subway to my brother's couch in Brooklyn seemed filled with stage laughter, even in its sad, nocturnal, and noisy silence.

Many years later, after moving to New York, I was there for *Cat on a Hot Tin Roof* and *Sweet Bird of Youth* and might have wondered what these steamy southern settings would ever have to do with me. Sensuous and seedy brass beds and sleepy overhead fans and women stripped to their slips, all seemed a long way from home. But I had gone and gone again, all the way up to the East Side production of *Suddenly Last Summer*. Cannibalism, no less. I think I had worked hard to reject any personal connection. But here I was saying, yes, I will try for Tennessee.

Part of it must have been the celebrity. After all, he was the most visible writer of his time. Hemingway had long gone, sucking death from the final pacifier, the nipplelike nozzle of a rifle. Mailer had tried to hog the headlines with many wives and too many advertisements for himself, a gifted user of words but words that lighted few ideas. Tennessee seemed to keep the dash-and-dot people of the gossip columns busy. In public he seemed simply outrageous, vying with Truman Capote for excesses on talk shows. (*Talk* and *show* always seemed to me to be two words that are in conflict.) I had myself seen him in deep-lined closeup being third-degreed by Mike Wallace on a local TV station before Wallace was accredited with dignity by being called a "correspondent" at CBS. I had seen him brutalized by the toothy inquisition of David Frost when he was asked, in those days when the closets were crowded and *gay* was still an adjective that meant "full of life and fun,"

5

whether he was a homosexual. He answered, "Oh, I cover the waterfront." And all America cheered, and they faded to a commercial message. Great fun. Well—maybe. I think America wanted to believe that a celebrity just had fun all the time. And when one blew his celebrated brains out, the *vox populi* moved on to another celebrity. Yes. Yes. Years later, Tennessee described it all to me as "the arena." Beginning his *celebrated* life was entering the arena. How many gorings would I witness?

Certainly he had earned his winnings. There was a time when even the critics had names that seemed as double-breasted as a thoughtful evening in a comfortable theater. In the *Times*, when reviews were still a kind of eloquent literature, Brooks Atkinson wrote about Tennessee:

> He possesses a terrifying knowledge of the secrets of the mind. . . . He is a poetic writer who could look through the polite surfaces of life into the pain that froze the hearts of lonely people.

Winner or loser, I thought not.
Ready or not, here I come.
I set out to secure one playwright of our time to be a subject. After all, what did all that stuff have to do with me?

> He knew the silent secrets of the mind. Tennessee often said that being sensitive brought its own terror. But being sensitive made life richer.

He had been through a recent hell and survived. The one lasting relationship of his life, with his own gentleman caller, his friend and lover of many years, Frank Merlo, had ended with a painful death by cancer. Remorse and pain agonized Tennessee. The many doctors had prescribed many pills, and the wine with which he downed them had made him into a chemical volcano. He had a passionate lust for life, but his childhood fear of illness left him starting the day, every day, with the announcement, "I am dying." Finally in 1969, when the inevitable explosion took place, his own brother Dakin, "the normal Williams" as he was sometimes called with a smile, had had him committed to a psychiatric hospital, where, he told me later, his only visitor had been his most talented director, Elia Kazan. It was a nightmare from which he was just awakening when I met him. Finally, out and reborn with a desire to try to go the distance again, his new play, then called *The Two-Character Play*, later *Out Cry*, the product of all that overwhelming fear and aloneness, was brutalized by the critics in Chicago; it died a quick death. There had been violent arguments with the little porcelain lady who was nonetheless a tigress at the theatrical gates, Audrey Wood; she had after all in many ways discovered Tennessee and brought him to the center stage of world fame and fortune as his agent. Their lives and fortunes had once blended, but now there was anger. Perhaps she failed to feel how much that play meant to Tennessee, who was now feeling that he was exploring new territory of the mind and theater. Their parting was like a personal earthquake for both.

Tennessee had been determined not to lose, but to win again. Start fresh, start new. International Creative Management was still anxious to hold him as a client. His prestige was worldwide. They assigned an eager young man to be his new agent, Bill Barnes. It was to him that I went, really unaware of the topography of the terrain of Tennessee. I went with my idea, no, my wife's idea, to make a film called *Tennessee Williams' South*.

Although God knows I was naïve, it seemed like a good, simple idea. After all, the South was rising from its long sleep. Martin Luther King had sung us his dream. And the Freedom Riders were marching on and could not be stopped. Who could have been better to guide us on film through a real time and place of revolution than Tennessee, the poet of the South? I called Bill Barnes on a Monday. He said to call back later in the week. It was a time full with appointments, but he was eager to please. Each day I called. Each day it seemed impossible. I knew I would have to return to Canada by the weekend; but my own childhood, deprived and depressed, has always made every "no" a personal challenge. I learned that Tennessee was as regular and passionate a swimmer as I was. I suggested to Bill Barnes that if necessary I would hold our first meeting in a pool or in the steam room afterward.

Friday morning I made my last call. Barnes said that Tennessee had been amused by my idea of meeting underwater. A lunch had been canceled; if I could make it, I could make my case personally to Tennessee. I would be the host. I was told to pick them up at the Elysée Hotel on East Fifty-fourth Street just after twelve. I rushed uptown wearing my Canadian sealskin cap and green loden coat. I mention what I was wearing because right from the start the whole experience took on a make-believe kind of theatricality. The doorman saluted me when I rushed out of the cab with a smile. He said, "You'll find your brother in the Monkey Bar, Mr. Williams."

What?

But I was too surprised and nervous to question. I thanked him and went to meet my "brother."

He greeted me with that constant nervous laugh. "Billy here tells me you're partial to steam rooms." And a laugh again.

And that stare: the eyes that pierce deeper than any I have ever known. If there is a soul, that was where he was reading me. I'm not surprised that Edwina, his mother, once said of him as a child, "Other children would pick a flower, then carelessly throw it away, but Tom would stand peering into the heart of the flower as though trying to discover the secret of life."

There was no turning back. And no hiding place, for either of us.

"I understand you're buying lunch, huh." And he laughed. I laughed in response, although I wasn't sure why at the time.

As we left the hotel to head down Madison Avenue to lunch, the doorman again saluted with the greeting, "Good morning, Mr. Williams and Mr. Williams' brother."

And a loud cackle from Tennessee as he raised his eyebrows to welcome the splendid air of madness that seemed to follow our particular parade.

I suppose we were something of a sight. My own seal cap, now a sentimental relic, had become ragged with time. And I knew I would never replace it, having seen photos of the murder of young seals. Tennessee was wearing a red-orange fur coat of uncertain origin. He seemed to like to accentuate his physical qualities with semi-self-mockery. In a short novel that he wrote soon afterward called *Moise and the World of Reason*, which seemed anything but

8

reasonable, he described one of the central characters as being clothed in a fur coat of some kind which made him look like a stunted bear or an overgrown muskrat. If passersby turned to stare, even in blasé New York, I would not have been surprised, but I can recall thinking, maybe we are like a pair of mad March Hares, but it is quite wonderful. There was an automatic connection.

I don't think his eyes left me during the entire lunch, a look of bemused contemplation. What was it I wanted? What is this man going to do to me? The scars of so many mishandlings were obvious; his heart was on his sleeve like a badge of courage.

"Baby," he said, "I been there, so many times before." He was referring to having been, as they say, "done" by television.

He said that he felt that he had been giving interviews all his life. He explained many times, in many ways, why he went back for more. He felt at times a sense of almost nonbeing, and thus a craving for recognition and a reassertion of his existence both as an artist and as a man. He admitted that he had been so often wrong about giving himself to editors and TV people, but he wanted to know what else he could do. New plays demanded new comments, new attention. He was both innocent and cynical if that is possible. And much that was impossible for others was standard life-style for him. He just had to let go, release his being on the world. For him, there seemed no other way but to be totally himself no matter what the consequences.

I like what the novelist Cynthia Ozick said in a recent essay on "literature lost." "Applause," she wisely noted, "is an anonymous act. Dissent never is."

He was a constant dissenter, even arguing with his past glory, striking out into the mind-space of the unknown.

He was the personification of what the English poet Edward Dyer meant back in the sixteenth century, "My mind to me a Kingdom is."

This was the state of mind he was in that day at lunch. I think I talked too fast and too much. I said that I was interested in the idea more than anything, not the gossip: I was after the spirit. I told him in some detail about the film on Shaw and how I had been able to find some of the world's most skilled actors, such as Christopher Plummer and Genevieve Bujold, to recreate scenes from his work. It was the poetry of the man I was after.

"What was that quote of Shaw's I like?" he asked. "Yuh know, about Rembrandt and beauty?"

Shaw was still much on my mind. I was able to rhyme it off. The quote was from a Shaw character trying to sum up a code of behavior, a wish for a style of life:

I believe in Michelangelo, Velasquez and Rembrandt, in the might of design, the mystery of colour, the redemption of all things by beauty everlasting, and the message of art that made these hands blessed.

Tennessee leaned on his elbow and looked at me thoughtfully. "I think I believe a lot of that. Yeh." He nodded approvingly. "Suppose we have a look at Harry's *Wit and World of G. Bernard Shaw*. Yeh. Suppose we do that."

So a start might be made. There was some business talk between Billy and Tennessee about the forthcoming opening of a new work called *Small Craft Warnings*, to open on Easter Sunday in 1972—an idea Tennessee did not favor. He said, "Somebody is bound to make a crack about the Resurrection. They'll say the Resurrection didn't come off." He laughed an Easter laugh. And there was talk of a birthday celebration that weekend. I was invited to drop by.

The party was one of those New York events where, because of an excess of "the beautiful people," you can only remember the presence of Andy Warhol, whom Tennessee described as being "so much like a lost little boy, lost in time." I was struck by Warhol's whiteness, pale face; a pale painter. Tennessee was, as always, polite. And Billy advised me that the screening of the Shaw film would have to take place in Los Angeles, where Tennessee was headed to be the presenter of an Oscar, after the opening. We were becoming a moveable feast.

So I entered his life. Prior to the screening, we met for drinks at the bar of the Polo Lounge of the Beverly Hills Hotel, perhaps the only place with any ongoing history in Hollywood. Gus the

"The South is where my head is." Tennessee in Jackson Park in New Orleans points to the geography of his mind.

The title of the film, using Tennessee Williams' signature.

Along the back roads of Mississippi, a silent black boy among the cotton fields of the South, a loner as Tennessee was as a child. "I always thought I was black," Tennessee said. "Where does he come from? Where does he go?"

The opening credit announces the film by Harry Rasky. The sunflower is a frequent symbol in Tennessee's work, growing in unexpected places under difficult situations, reaching for the source of life, the sun itself.

Along the streets of New Orleans where he first found free-dom, Tennessee walks to a jazz beat. He loved the language of jazz.

On the patio of his house in Key West, he announces that he is an angry old man, facing a world that has disappointed him. He was the poet of passion.

Remembering his grandparents in New Orleans. They gave his childhood joy. His father provided the phrase "Cat on a Hot Tin Roof," a phrase used to describe his nervous condition when his wife began to nag as he came in the door.

The many watches of a sales-
man who has been on the
road and been rewarded.
Burl Ives proud of the gifts of
admirers in a scene filmed in
Key West.

Burl Ives is still
the personification of
Big Daddy.

A day of brooding at sea. Tennessee remembering the unhappy life of his father who drank too much. The sweet bird of youth has flown away.

Harry Rasky interviews Tennessee Williams in one of the many conversations filmed over a period of a year.

Greek, probably the world's best bartender, who has been a silent witness to the rise and fall of more show-business moguls and midgets than any man alive, was pouring. Billy proudly had in his hand a set of the reviews of *Small Craft Warnings*. This was still a time before the critics totally wasted Tennessee. The reviews raved more about the past than the present. There was only the early rumor of what Tennessee was later to categorize as "the perhaps."

Clive Barnes, before he was demoted from his command post at *The New York Times*, scattered slightly tattered bouquets of kindness.

> Williams is a writer of enormous compassion. . . . a compassion that opens up doors into bleak and empty hearts. . . . [*Small Craft Warnings*] has a seedy honesty . . . a feel for the waste of life and also for the human spirit for survival.

Richard Watts, one of his more solid supporters, provided hope:

> Contains some of his most characteristically eloquent writing and compassionate portraits of lost and brooding souls and it is proof that the distinguished playwright hasn't lost his touch.

And T. E. Kalem wanted us to know in *Time* magazine that the poet had indeed not lost his touch.

> To these characters, the bar is a spar to which they cling in the shipwreck of existence and over which they confess their hidden better selves. These confessional arias are what they have always been in Williams, eloquent tributes to the English tongue and moving explorations of the human spirit. This is not to say that *Small Craft Warnings* is on a par with the durable canon of his finest plays. Here he reminds of the size and scope of his genius, but displays it diminuendo. Call this then a five-finger exercise from the man who is the greatest living playwright in the Western World.

Of course, it depended more on who was reading the reviews than who was writing them. Billy, always enthusiastic, was underlining "greatest living playwright." Tennessee was feeling the pain that would now gather force with each new opening and closing, aware that his career was being reviewed, not his play. He raised his glass to Gus and toasted, "To the body." He half turned to me, "Yuh see, Harry, they're waiting for the body." A loud laugh.

We were waiting for the Professor, who now arrived. Oliver Evans was referred to always as "my dearest, oldest friend" and was simply called "the Professor." I had been alerted that he had had an operation for brain cancer and perhaps did not have long to live. I was told by Tennessee to look deep into his eyes and I would see the terror of the future there. He had come in from the Valley, where he was teaching English at San Fernando Valley College, for the screening. He seemed both kind and courtly, in the mold of Tennessee himself, a southern gentleman. His hair was all gone from cobalt treatments. So it was difficult to discern his age. But I guessed that he and Tennessee were contemporaries, both veterans of "the Knightly Quest," with mutual memories of cruising some of the more-and-less exotic places of the secret garden of the gay world. I never did see Tennessee more at ease with anyone than he was with the Professor. They were like two old warriors together, proud of their romantic wars and wounds.

We adjourned to the private basement screening room of the Beverly Hills Hotel, which is the only film theater I am aware of that allows you to order room service. Many a difficult screening there has begun with champagne and ended with a hangover. Glasses and a light California Chablis arrived, and GBS was suitably toasted, even if he himself was a teetotaler, but I think considering the company he would not have insisted on an evening of temperance. My brother Eddy, who was a high school teacher in the Los Angeles system, and his exuberant wife Sonny also attended, and I noted how patient and thoughtful Tennessee was when Eddy talked with some enthusiasm about an amateur school production of *The Glass Menagerie*.

Now it was time for the unveiling, introducing to one another, in my way, two of the great forces of theater in the century. They were well met.

As the lights were coming on after the screening, Tennessee touched my arm tenderly and said, "You've shown me a part of

Shaw I never knew." It was a gentle and well-meant compliment. And then he stood, as if for the gathered crowd, and raised his glass to the now-blank screen. "To all playwrights, now and forever."

Oliver Evans, the Professor, joined in the praise and suggested that Tennessee return with him to spend the night at his home in the Valley. Tennessee said to me, "If you want the real story, Harry, you'd better come along. Hah! The Professor has the real story." I was flattered that Tennessee would include me, which he now would, in fact, at most major events that took place over the next decade. It was almost as if he had chosen me to be there, to be a camera, to bear witness. I had thought until recently that I had selected him; not quite so, or only partly so. The laughter and lamentation would now slowly erode any artificial professional barrier. "Jump in, baby, this is only the start." And so we went to the Valley.

I cannot recall if Robert, or was it Victor, also came. There was always a Robert or Victor, some blond young man of twenty-five or so, with wide shoulders and not much to say, who was introduced more or less as Tennessee's "secretary" or "companion." In moments of serious discussion about theater or film or ideas, Tennessee would talk over him as if he were a mere shadow on the table. If he left the room, Tennessee would raise his eyebrows as if to say, "Sorry, I need them." He did not travel well alone. There were certain things he could not do with ease, such as drive, make coffee or phone calls, or really find his way. Strange as that may sound, these constant young men were the always present nonpresent, if you know what I mean.

As so many meetings with Tennessee did, this evening had its share of reality and symbolism. It seemed to be both happening and a fantasy at the same time, if that is possible. Here was the world's most famous and perhaps wealthiest playwright abandoning his superdeluxe suite at the epitome of comfort, the Beverly Hills Hotel, to spend the night on the cot of a rather threadbare house in the confined blockhouse of the poverty-stricken Professor. The house looked about as substantial as a California Christmas-tree decoration.

Tennessee either pretended not to notice or did not notice as Oliver Evans opened his mostly empty refrigerator to produce a half-gallon bottle of Gallo, less-than-table-quality wine. The wine and ideas flowed. It was the closest I can recall Tennessee coming to having an intellectual evening involving his own work and the work of others. He had enormous respect for the Professor. There was a little verbal horseplay about my "straightness" but never enough to cause me any distress. It was now assumed that I would move into his life to observe anything and everything. It was not absolute trust, because Tennessee was too paranoid for that as I would find out later, but he also hated "mendacity" (a Big Daddy word that he liked), and if he was going to reveal himself, it would be emotionally naked with no shame, no "mendacity."

At first there was talk about the recent suicide of the famous Japanese writer Yukio Mishima, who fell purposely on his sword. Tennessee and the Professor had known him and visited him recently, perhaps in the bar of a Tokyo hotel.

"It was his body," said Tennessee, "his body. His sensibility would not allow him to watch it decay. The Orientals know how to end it themselves, quickly. I may have to wait for a plane crash." There was another loud, self-mocking laugh.

I asked if it was important to have his work remembered, certain that Tennessee's monument would be the largest for any playwright of our time. He said with some seriousness, "When I'm dead I wouldn't have any idea of whether my work is remembered or whether it was completely forgotten. So how could it make a particle of difference to me? Well, I think I really feel that, I'm concerned very much with how people react to it while I'm living. Yes. Because then it can affect me. But after my death, it can't possibly affect me one way or the other. Is that a selfish point of view? I don't know. Of course, on the whole I'm sure that in the back of my mind I hope that something will be remembered."

I nervously offered, "Well, I'm sure the plays will be remembered."

He said, "Well, thanks for the reassurance, Harry, but I don't think it's going to make much difference to me."

When Tennessee went into the other room, the Professor and I had an opportunity to talk. He commented again on how he liked the Shaw film and how well I had related the man to his work and family; he said he felt certain I would do the same with Tennessee.

But he warned, "Tennessee can be quite touchy about his work. He's usually suspicious of being psychoanalyzed—and with good reason, I might add. He's always regarded professional criticism with something only less than contempt. About his family too he can be touchy, though he does not spare the lash in discussing them informally. I have always felt there was a situation in his own family that accounted for his feeling about the dependency upon relatives he writes about in his plays. I have never dared to inquire. He may be franker with you, whom he knows less well, as paradoxically is often the case."

The Professor went on to describe this family dependency, which he was also to amplify later in a letter. He said:

You may have noticed that one of Tennessee's most characteristic obsessions concerns the plight of persons dependent upon their—usually unwilling—relatives for their maintenance. I suppose *Streetcar* is the first important play to reveal this obsession, though it is present in several of the early one-acters. He has always been particularly concerned about this type of situation, which, of course, provides him with opportunity for the compassion that is the hallmark of his drama and—I've always been convinced—that has also been a very large factor, perhaps the largest, in his greatness. The defeated and the mutilated are those characters whom we remember best, and I think this holds true for the entire body of his work, though it's especially conspicuous in the early and late plays. It's *least* true of the plays he wrote at the height of his fame, so there is very likely a large amount of self-identification involved: his insecurity at the beginning of his career and his current fears concerning what he regards as the waning of his creative powers.

Tennessee reentered, rather playfully. "Well, I didn't know whether I dared leave you two alone. Hah hah."

How much of what he said and did was prearranged in his mind and how much was just existence was not clear then or even now. But it was almost as if a director were chalking our positions for a play that was about to begin (or for a life that was coming to an end).

The next day some things became clearer.

15

*　　*　　*

Tennessee and I met at about one P.M. at the pool in the Beverly Hills Hotel. We watched an attractive young couple come down the winding staircase that allows starlets to make suitable entrances.

"How very attractive," Tennessee said.

"She is pretty," I said.

"No. I mean him. Hah hah."

Not quite knowing what to say, I said something lame like, "Well, people may not be what they seem."

"Well, Harry, hah hah, that's what we're going to find out—about you."

He dove into the pool and swam rapidly away, not waiting for, nor perhaps even expecting, an answer.

I swam my lengths in silence. Tennessee was ahead of me, always ahead of me. When I surfaced, he was gone. I was troubled. Billy Barnes came to see me.

"Tennessee liked your Shaw film. So did I, and so did the Professor. He is quite prepared to go ahead with the film."

Of course I was pleased, even though I had suspected this was the case from the evening before. But I was stopped by what Billy now added.

"Oliver Evans will be the paid consultant. He will have Tennessee's five-thousand-dollar fee. Tennessee wants to give him money to go to the Orient for one last trip. Oliver wants to go to the Orient to die. He has no money. Tennessee wants him to go with dignity."

I said, "That seems all right to me. But that is very high for a consultant on this kind of film. I was not planning on hiring anyone."

"Tennessee insists that be the condition," Billy said.

And so our dance of reality-fantasy fiction-fact gracefully did a two-step. The Professor's measured thought from the evening before about the "reluctant dependent relative" took on new meaning. The "defeated" and the "mutilated," the bond of brotherhood and the brain-scarred, somehow were working their way into a fragment of the film not yet begun.

"No problem," I said to Billy Barnes, with both lamentation and laughter.

*　　*　　*

16

Back in my city of Toronto, I was now about to try to convince the conservative Canadian Broadcasting Corporation, which was trying to focus on Canadian national heroes, that it should do a film about a Southern American writer whose reviews were slipping and whose personal exploits seemed to be making more space in *Playboy* than in the literary reviews. And after doing this, I was to advise the even more conservative CBC contract-legal department that five thousand dollars were immediately to be sent to an obscure Professor who would confer by mail from Borneo—that is, if he lived.

The program director of the time, an imaginative fellow called Thom Benson, was an early supporter. He sent the request up the bureaucratic ladder. It came clanking back down with the comment, "Why should we be doing a film about Tennessee Ernie Ford? What does he mean to Canada?"

Trouble.

My street sense was aroused. Since the BBC had been involved in my earlier Shaw film, I phoned the head of BBC "features" in London to see if he would consider coming in as a partner in this worthy enterprise. I was advised that he would. I was reassured by this, even if later it would turn out that his verbal agreement wasn't, in the immortal words of that philosopher Samuel Goldwyn, "worth the paper it was written on."

But at the time the BBC promise gave me the courage to proceed without formal approval from various CBC bureaucrats. I discovered that travel forms could be issued and a crew could be assigned without too many sets of the sacred bureaucratic initials. I booked a crew to New Orleans to start filming. And so off we flew. After all, what could possibly stop us now?

Naturally, there was no way any enterprise involving Tennessee could go smoothly. In changing planes at Buffalo, the order came that all baggage was to be off-loaded. My first thought was that the bureaucrats had caught me. I then thought it was because they had discovered that we were filming Tennessee and the drug squad was after us. (Paranoia is contagious.) As we found, it was one of those rare spot customs checks; but with a ton or more of equipment, it was no easy matter. The situation was further confounded by an overanxious customs commando who spotted what he considered to be a false bottom in one case of our equipment. He wanted to

17

pry it open, even if it meant that we would miss our connecting flight. It was all we could do to convince him that it was in fact a special padded section built on to cushion the lighting equipment against airport handling or mishandling. With minutes to go, we were able to catch the flight. As Bryan Robertson, my fey unit manager, said, "Here we go on an airplane called Perspire." And "The Milk Plane Doesn't Stop Here Anymore."

Hah hah!

And I gave my heart to know wisdom, and to know madness and folly: I perceived that this also is vexation of spirit. For in much wisdom is much grief: and he that increaseth knowledge increaseth sorrow.

Eccles. 1:17–18

Tennessee's greeting for us in New Orleans was free and friendly. He seemed almost eager to talk and walk through his life. After a brief interlude of coffee and chicory, we adjourned to Jackson Park on a warm spring day. He wore a "revolutionary" tam and was sporting a goatee at the time, which he later admitted was a nuisance because he constantly was having to add black dye. ("Yuh know, like *Death in Venice*, that kind of thing. Huh?") We sat on folding lawn chairs, about to begin a picnic of which his existence was to be the dish of the day.

And then it began. "Sound roll one, Tennessee Williams. Picture one. Harry Rasky, director." The transcript lists a second request to start because of "wild talking." I had meant to lead Tennessee gently down the road of his past and to have him guide us through the South in general. But from the start, he was to take me much further when I asked him to describe his South. He said, "Can I describe it? Well, I think I've been working at it for a long time. Hah hah. Trying to describe it. It sometimes seemed to me that I inhabit my own country. It's where my head is, I guess, as the kids say today."

It became clear that this would be a journey that would never end, as it went deeper and deeper into his life and the areas of all our lives where we seldom care to or dare to explore. "His country" is the raw and tender territory within us. Who has the courage to

18

explore there? I recall Brooks Atkinson writing about *A Streetcar Named Desire*, "People came away from it profoundly moved and also in some curious way elated. For they have been sitting all evening in the presence of truth and that is a rare and wonderful experience. Out of nothing more esoteric than interest in human beings, Mr. Williams has looked steadily and wholly into the private agony of the lost person."

His South was real but universal. In it he constructed a microcosm of all experience. I prodded him to tell me how the plays could be so universal if they are all located in one place. He said patiently, "Oh, I don't think of myself as a regional writer. I think the choice of southern locale is just because I find it a good background for the drama of relationships and existences, yuh know. That's what interests me."

Later, the Professor, Oliver Evans, in his long-distance role as consultant (maybe we should have called him "consultant-at-large"), sent me his thoughts about the relationship of the locale to the characters. The letter was mailed from Pattaya Beach, Thailand.

No other playwright has so thoroughly explored that area of the country. And the type of character in whom he has specialized and made famous are, of course, women characters who embody many of the attitudes that made it such an interesting place to live in (by *it* I mean of course the South, especially the Delta region) in the Thirties and Forties, when there was still some local color that was unselfconscious. A Blanche is not met down there very easily nowadays; I suppose because it's been such a long time since places like Belle Reve have ceased to exist except as tourist attractions.

The truth is that Tennessee delights in showing us people of both sexes who have reached the end of their respective ropes in various ways—people who are lonely, trapped, and desperate. If he can be said to have a single major theme, it is surely this one. And it is true that the South, with its tragic history and its poverty and the disorientation that, after all these years, still prevails there, makes an ideal setting for the depiction of individual catastrophes that mirror the general plight and the socio-cultural scene as a whole. I think this is something you might emphasize, nor have I ever read, in any Williams criticism, this so-obvious relationship between the locale of his plays and the predicaments in which their characters so frequently find themselves.

That morning in Jackson Park, I asked him if in *A Streetcar Named Desire* Blanche represented the South. He said, "Oh, very much so. Very much, yeh. Blanche is a typical southern lady in some respects."

I asked if Blanche's poetic nature was a southern trait, a southern characteristic. He looked into the hot morning sun and said, "Yes, southerners express themselves much more lyrically, especially the women. Now, you even take southern politicians, they express themselves quite colorfully, compared to the northern politicians, don't you think? They have a very picturesque turn of phrase and a great many of them talk with a sort of rhetoric that I used for Big Daddy in *Cat on a Hot Tin Roof*, yuh know. My father had a great gift of idiom, it seemed to me."

Of course, I wanted to know where Tennessee felt that came from. What was the source?

"Most of it comes from the blacks, yuh know," he said, thoughtfully running his finger across his trimmed beard. "A great many of our idioms come from the blacks. The title "Cat on a Hot Tin Roof," for instance, was a favorite phrase of my father's, and when he would come home and mother would go after him for his conditions, he would say, 'Edwina, cut it out, you're making me as nervous as a cat on a hot tin roof.' Hah hah. When she would reproach him for his condition when he came in the door. Hah hah."

He had written frequently about human emotion and his own personal involvement, and I wanted to know more about it. He had made a point of saying frequently that when he attacked the human race he was also including himself because he, too, was part of the pack. He said he did not regard himself as superior in any way. He said that it was impossible to write about human frailty unless he, too, was a victim of it. He admitted to having exposed a great number of human foibles and brutishness, but he said he was talking also of himself. He was a test tube of the extreme.

*   *   *

20

"Who wins," I asked, "in the battle between the brute and the poet? Is the brute within us always trying to conquer the poet?"

"I wouldn't say strictly the poet. I don't . . . I've only written about poets twice. I don't think the qualities of being sensitive are strictly and solely the possession of people who practice the art of poetry. I think these people are moved primarily by gentle emotions, sensibility, you know, rather than . . . But then I always, when I start talking like this, I always become very suspicious of myself. I don't know."

He stopped himself with a larger-than-usual nervous laugh, as if he were surprised at the tone of the conversation, exploring more philosophical than personal matters. He had been hammered too long, too deeply, too disappointedly by the popular press that wanted new details of the strange personal interludes in his life. But he seemed to appreciate, even if apprehensively, the area under discussion.

He said, "It doesn't sound right. It sounds like I was delivering some sort of lecture for which I was not prepared."

I thought I would try to dig deeper into the question of violence, which seemed to come up a number of times in reviews of his work.

"Is the South different from the American North in terms of its attitude towards violence, would you say?"

He answered, "Wouldn't you say that violence was about equally present? There's a great deal of violence in great cities like New York. Didn't you encounter personal violence in New York?"

He was referring to an encounter I had had and written about in a story called "The Chain," in which a large black man mugged me without apparent reason in New York a couple of years before. I had told him about my pain. Tennessee never forgot any personal message. It was always as if his antennae were reaching out to souls around him. He felt their hurts and their longings. He said, "I've never encountered any violence in the South myself. Me, personally. I never have. I think there must be something forbidding in my aspect, despite my shortness of stature."

Again, a loud self-deprecating laugh as he imagined his five-foot-six body against the forces of violence. It amused him. "Hah hah. You can see me against those violently inclined, can't you, Harry?"

Yes, I could, as time passed, see him against the world.

Now deeper into himself, as if he were searching in areas not easily visible even to himself, he added, "Yuh know, I never struck anyone. I never had an inclination to. Still, I think I have a violent, a very emotional nature."

In preparing myself, I had read of his love for the peacefulness of his childhood surroundings. He had talked of Mississippi as a dark, wide, open world that you can breathe in. That breath had come so much, I knew, from his grandparents. I asked, "In your childhood in the South, your grandparents were an enormous influence, correct?"

The sun was shaded behind a huge magnolia tree, and for the first time he seemed almost serene. For those few minutes of conversation, memory had taken hold and memory brought calm. He said, sweetly—yes, sweetly—"Yeh, they were archetypes of the gentle ones, yuh know, they were the gentlest and sweetest people I've ever known and they still are. After sixty-one years of life, they remain the sweetest and gentlest two people I've ever known, and it isn't merely a familial bias, I don't think. They literally were."

"Were they necessarily creatures of the South?"

He objected quickly. "No, no, no. My grandfather Dakin was of Quaker ancestry from Ohio. He and my grandmother were married in Ohio. They came south when they were still young to teach school in eastern Tennessee. And my grandmother was head of the music department. A very beautiful woman. I have a picture of her I'll show you while you're here. She taught violin and piano and we lived under rather stringent circumstances. My grandmother was always providing us with a little spending money that she saved from her music pupils. It was all the spending money we had as children."

I recalled a story he had written about his grandmother called "Grand."

He half-closed his eyes as if to see her face again. "Yes, I did. Yeh. I wrote about her practicing and contributing to the family upkeep, such as it was."

His description of her was like gentle, warm rain.

He had always called her "Grand." And he meant it. He looked forward to her visits as if waiting for a fine soft music. To him she was the South personified, with its remembered grace and charmed laughter. Her time with him was in such contrast to the family tension, with the spoken and unspoken anger of his mother and father. She represented the free fields of childhood in contrast to the confined apartment of a gray city and its claustrophobic land-scapes.

As he grew older, she was as much imagination as reality, and he thought of her representing God in his and his sister's life.

His grandfather, adding to the homemade legend, reminded him that she was born on All Souls' Day and that she died on the Feast of Epiphany. So she became almost a family saint.

He regretted her passing before he had found fame and was able somehow to justify the gifts she had given him. She was like soft cotton and kindness.

Among the famous men of the world I have filmed, it is a recurring theme in describing areas of disappointment that a loved parent or grandparent was not able to live to see fame and accom-plishment bestowed on the once-child graced with kindness. Jack Benny, the comedian, told me that that was what he regretted most— the fact that his father had never known the achievement of his son. Marc Chagall, the painter, similarly said that that was the source of his inner strength, the love that his mother had given him as a child, and he was still, in a way, trying to honor the memory of his mother, who had not lived to see the day of his fame.

Tennessee's grandfather had been there for some time. He lived to his mid-nineties and was a traveling companion. They were fellow travelers in time. At sixteen, Tennessee was allowed to go along while his grandfather conducted a tour of ladies through Europe, a voyage he described as being "very Scott and Zelda Fitzgerald." It was also a trip of enormous spiritual self-revelation. It was little wonder that the grandfather emerged in some form in Tennessee's work. I asked if in fact his grandfather was a prototype for the character Nonno in *The Night of the Iguana*.

He responded with some enthusiasm: "Very much so. Except that he was not a professional poet. He loved poetry. He was always reciting it. He would recite 'The Raven' by heart, yuh know, 'The Raven' and quite a few poems. He used to read it aloud to my grandmother, but she would fall asleep. He found that she didn't appreciate poetry very much. He said it was because she was a poem herself." He punctuated the end of this episode with one of his laughs. As if to say, let's move on, out of my memory for a while, please, it hurts.

It was approaching noon, and the park was alive with the mix of laughter and music that is a constant sound of New Orleans. I tried to get us back to the real South. It was my first trip to New Orleans, and I felt a great ease there. And I said that the whites and the blacks seemed harmonious there.

He said, "Yeh, that's always been peculiar to New Orleans. When I first came here in the late thirties, I noticed how well they lived together. They lived side by side in the French Quarter and there was never any discomfort among them about it, yuh know. They accepted each other's presence quite amicably. This racial tension has grown in the South only in the last decade, I think. I think it's going to work itself out, yuh know. I hope without violence. Of course, the things that have happened in the last couple of days are frightening [referring to the attempted assassination on Governor Wallace]. One can only be happy that it was a white apparently who shot Governor Wallace. People told me there would have been a bloodbath here and in other Southern cities if it had been a black, yuh know, who'd done it."

"Don't you think it's true that the whites and the blacks live together more closely in the South than they do in the North?"

"Well, yes, they do. Of course, southerners are brought up among blacks. For instance, usually southerners have black nurses. And actually there's a warmer feeling toward blacks in the South than there is in the North, where the black is relatively a stranger to them, you know."

I asked, "Do you think that that's still true today, given the rise of the Black Panthers and that sort of thing?"

"It's becoming less true, don't you think? I do think that the black part of our population is quite justified in its, well, let's say restlessness, and its feeling of dissent, political dissent, because I think they have lived under pretty intolerable inequities, mostly economic. And these things will have to resolve themselves if the world doesn't destroy itself in the next couple of decades. I expect

Remembering God, stating his belief. "God is a good word, a short one."

John Colicos plays the priest with Colleen Dewhurst in The Night of the Iguana, *filmed outside Colleen's summer house in New England.*

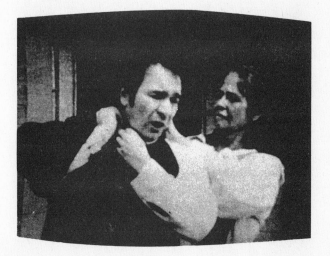

Colleen tries to paint the haunted eyes of the priest in The Night of the Iguana, *but finds there is too much suffering in them.*

Tennessee toasts eccentrics everywhere during some sidewalk filming on the streets of New Orleans.

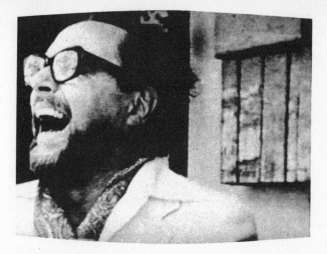

His famous laugh. In his dialogue with Harry Rasky, Tennessee enjoys the pleasure of knowing that all people are eccentric.

Splendid Canadian Shakespearean actor William Hutt in a scene from Small Craft Warnings *filmed in Stratford, Ontario.*

Tennessee plays for the camera. Reading a humorous poem about how people burn to death out of boredom, listening to each other's life story, he finds a suitable robe and enjoys ''shocking'' the crew.

Rasky and Tennessee as they walk through the French Quarter of New Orleans in search of the street named Desire.

In the garden of his apartment home in New Orleans announcing that he is "both Stanley and Blanche."

Brilliant actress, Jessica Tandy, recreates for the camera a speech from A Streetcar Named Desire. *It is staged in Tennessee's patio in Key West to provide a certain theatrical musical reality. Jessica is still the Blanche against which every actress must be judged.*

Jessica Tandy in Tennessee's chair in Key West plays Blanche, pleading with the audience to recognize the progress of civilization in one of Tennessee's greatest speeches.

Tennessee reads his poem of the moths on a street in New Orleans. Blanche, he says, was like a giant tiger moth.

Once again, the theme of ''Where does he come from? Where does he go?''

to see the whites and the blacks in America beginning to merge into each other, and out of it I think will come a much greater race of people."

It seemed to me that we were on serious ground and that Tennessee's dream was the same as Martin Luther King's. I wanted to explore further. I asked, "There seems to be a note of optimism in your work. Someone said that in your work the most important thing is the idea that man will save himself through compassion for each other."

"Yes," he said quickly, "yes, if he saves himself at all, it will be through comprehension."

"Would you be optimistic about that?"

He reflected. "I don't see how the human race will ever quite go through the act of total self-destruction. I think the will to survive is too deeply rooted in us for us to ever have this great confrontation of great nuclear powers. No, I don't think it will happen."

The transcript of those events lists "wild talking," and then "tape cuts," followed by the end of "roll one." On that note of optimism and the now-blistering noon sun, I felt the morning picnic should terminate for lunch. Tennessee suggested we all lunch together. It was a jovial repast. During the meal, he looked each member of the crew in the eyes, deeply in the eyes, and found some characteristic to comment on. With the exception of only one or two others, such as Arthur Miller and Teresa Stratas, I've never known a subject to be so aware of the ordinary worker. He had written elsewhere about the danger of success: "Maids, waiters, bellhops, porters and so forth are the most embarrassing people in the world for they continually remind you of the inequities which we accept as the proper thing. . . . Nobody should have to clean up anybody else's mess in the world." (Amen!)

I was so pleased with our first morning's productive output that I suggested to my unit manager that he send a telegram to our headquarters in Toronto indicating that our filming was going extremely well. The crew members asked for a short pause after lunch so that each could buy a volume of Tennessee's work to be autographed.

After lunch, he seemed eager to begin. We set up the camera in the courtyard of his apartment house. The small building was his investment. It was being managed at the moment by young Victor, who seemed most eager to show off his new gadget, a radio that was tuned in to a weather station to let you know the weather every second of the day. Tennessee raised his eyebrows, beseeching me for perhaps a little understanding as Victor vanished somewhere under an overhead fan, listening to reports of distant thunder. Tennessee was fond of stray cats, dogs, and humans. His ancient Boston terrier bitch named Gigi waddled by behind us, and the cat called Gentleman Caller settled down under a chair to escape the scorching sun, which seemed to be bleaching Tennessee's white linen suit even whiter. It was a Sahara-like afternoon, and time for questions.

In *Camino Real* he wrote about the unanswered question of life and the importance and dignity of asking the question. The questions now would become literary. Others' works. His own works. I reminded him that George Bernard Shaw had said that he "stood on the shoulders of Shakespeare" and that he admired Ibsen among more recent writers. I asked Tennessee who besides Shaw, whom we had talked a great deal about because of my film, had most influenced his work.

His answer was quick. "Oh, I think the most moving writer to me that ever lived was Chekhov, personally. His works have been a fetish with me. Chekhov. I read everything about him I can find. I love his letters, his journals and, of course, his theater. Yuh know, I spent a whole summer in 1934 reading Chekhov short stories at my grandparents' home in Memphis."

"Do you think that your locale, the South, is similar to Chekhov's?"

"Very much. Very much, like czarist Russia."

"But it changed. Is the South changing in the same way?"

"Oh, I think the South cannot resist change. Although it would very much like to believe still in *Gone with the Wind*."

"But then," I said, "one of your most moving plays is *The Glass Menagerie*. It's not set in the South. It's set in St. Louis."

He brushed his finger across his beard. "That's true. Yeh. It was set in St. Louis, where my sister and I had such a difficult time. It is by no means a southern city. It's a typical midwestern urban city in what they call the "heartland" of America. Hah hah hah! . . . which we found rather *heartless*, you might say."

26

I had heard Tennessee do a reading for a small recording company. I asked him now to read the introduction to *The Glass Menagerie*.

"All right," he said, "I'll change my glasses and give it a try." The childhood eye injury and the cataracts that had followed and the many eye operations were the curse of his life, in a way, and the death of him, in a more exact way. He changed his glasses and began thumbing through the pocket edition of the play that we had brought along. He studied the early pages of the book. "Oh, my gosh, there's a lot of peripheral material here. Hmmm. I think the stage . . . the description of the stage apartment is probably better than the play." And he let go with a loud laugh. But then there was the reading. It was as if a warm tropical wind had caught us all. Yes, we could feel the pain. No actor ever delivered that soliloquy with that feeling, like a memory that haunts through sleeping and daylight hours. Images floating about like a bar of music that catches your subconscious unawares.

I don't know if anyone who has not felt deeply or painfully, constantly agonizing over his condition, over the human condition, could ever give those lines that introduce that play the same poetic magic. I was frankly so caught in the moment of the aria that I lost my way in the questioning, not knowing which road to follow. I asked, "The man who said hello and goodbye but sent no address. Is that something like you today . . . sort of wandering around like a—"

He interrupted me and said, "I would reckon so. I guess that even then I knew that I was my father, or his spitting image. Hah."

Although I had become used to his nervous laugh, this time I was somewhat shaken; his answer startled me because I had assumed from reading his mother's account that his father was not anyone he cared to suggest he shared anything in common with. In fact, *Remember Me to Tom*, her book, is almost totally dedicated to insisting that the blame for every misfortune she and Tennessee ever encountered was the fault of Tennessee's father. He must have had many a singed area, that "cat on a hot tin roof."

I tried to shift mental gears again, now wishing to switch to all our "fathers." I asked, "Talking about the image of one's father, do you find a kind of religious feeling in your work?"

27

But Tennessee was still fixed on his much-abused father.

"My father had absolutely no belief in religion whatsoever. I'm afraid I differ from him very much in that respect. I'm not religious in the conventional sense. But I am religious, I think."

I was not surprised, of course. His grandfather, a preacher, was such a strong force. I had read about Tennessee's conversion to Catholicism in the mental hospital, inspired by his brother. But I still could not quite see this marvelously rebellious spirit locked into any formal dogma. To challenge him, I asked him if he thought we were part of original sin, in search of redemption.

That brought a full-bodied laugh. "Heavens, no. No. That's all a crock of you-know-what."

I do not recall Tennessee ever using profanity while I was around. And it may be worth noting that, except for his very last works, despite talk of violence of every kind, there is no profanity in his writing. I think he had too high a regard for the subtlety of language to debase it with the easy shocker that has become so common now in the theater of today. And of course, profanity no longer causes any shock. Every ten-year-old knows the words.

His answer to my question about his religion was one of the most spiritual in all the conversations and would become an important and powerful segment of the film.

His thick glasses caught the afternoon sun and reflected it as if he were more connected with the universe around him than usual.

"My religion? Well, I never defined it precisely to myself. And it's more difficult to define it to people, except that I know—and I've said this often—in times of distress I pray. I don't think of God as somebody listening to individual appeals. But I think the act of praying brings solace."

I asked, "The priest in *The Night of the Iguana*, do you relate to his feeling about God as he describes it?"

He seemed pleased at the suggestion. "Oh, yeh. Very much. Yeh. You mean that he is connected with the elements. Yeh. With the naked elements. Yeh. I think back of existence there has to be a creative force. Otherwise, there could be no existence. Something has to have created existence. And just like, yuh know, the plainest kind of geometry, consequently there is a creative force. So we couldn't exist otherwise. Nothing could exist. And so you may call him God. It's a good word, a short one."

I don't know if he had ever phrased his thoughts quite that way. But the idea that God is a good word and a short one seemed to me an instant epigram. I asked him if he would now read the poem of the old man, the old man who was so much his grandfather, from *The Night of the Iguana*.

He wanted to apologize for the poem. He said, "Yes. Now, let me say that this poem belongs in the context of the play. It is a very early poem of mine. I remember writing it on the verandah of a hotel in Mexico, in Acapulco, which no longer exists. I wrote the poem there and that's where the old man, Nonno, composed it. It's just a minor poem like he would have written, I think."

Of course, the poem is a major work, still not totally grasped, as are so many of his poems. His own grandfather felt that Tennessee might be remembered more as a poet than as a playwright. Perhaps.

When the poem was finished, he let out one of his laughs and said, "I wish I liked that poem. Hah!"

The last line of the poem contained the phrase "the frightened heart of me." I said that, being in New Orleans, the phrase reminded me of Blanche.

"It's a very sentimental poem," he said.

I asked him now if he would describe the character of Blanche in *A Streetcar Named Desire*.

He began as if talking of a friend or neighbor whom he liked but had not seen recently, and wondered how she was getting along, a neighbor he rather liked but who was very complicated. "Oh, Blanche. She was not a great intellect, I think. Hah. But she had a great sensibility, I believe, great feeling. I think she was a neurotic, yuh know. But I saw that play recently in Milwaukee, or the University of Minnesota, and the part was done by a twenty-four-year-old girl. She played it for a great deal of comedy. And Blanche had a great deal of humor, yuh know. That's what redeems her from her posturing and her sentimentalizing. The humor of Blanche came through very beautifully there."

Since we were talking about this friend he had not seen in a while, I asked, "Could Blanche survive today?"

29

He smiled at the question. "Could she survive today? I'm not sure she would even exist today."

"Why?"

He began to debate somewhat whether one might encounter Blanche if one turned the next corner. "I'm not sure she would exist because the South has changed so very much. Well, maybe she would. I have met many southern ladies with all kinds of romantic pretensions. But underneath Blanche's pretensions was something genuinely sensitive and tender. So many of these southern ladies that I meet nowadays with these Garden District airs and their plantation niceties of behavior—hah. You find them hard as nails underneath."

We seemed to be getting closer to Blanche, and I reminded him that he had once said that she was a tigress underneath.

He said, "Yes, she was. She was a strong weak person. A very strong weak person. I don't mean that to be a totally nonsensical thing to say. A person is either strong or weak. I would say she was strong, wouldn't you? She was predominantly strong. But with the odds in her disfavor, the odds against her."

As one who has always been moved and disturbed, powerfully disturbed, at the painful mental end of Blanche, I couldn't help but ask the creator of the character, the very real person, "Why did she have to go mad?"

He seemed surprised at the question. "Why did she have to go what?"

"Mad," I repeated.

"Mad! Because the odds were so heavily weighed against her and she had to expiate the death of her husband. She felt she had destroyed him by her failure to comprehend him. She called him 'disgusting,' yuh know."

And so in the middle of the afternoon we debated the behavior of Tennessee's people, as if perhaps that night in some local theater Blanche would perhaps meet with some happy ending or, listening in, she might exit to her fate with a greater understanding of what went wrong. I asked him if her fate had to do with "redemption or this religious notion of behavior."

He said, "I think we're all quite guilt-ridden, yuh know, deeply. If we have a capacity for guilt, I think we're quite guilt-ridden.

Certainly I am, and most people I know are to some extent. It's a puritanical thing, to some extent. Don't you think?"

I suppose I did agree. My own Orthodox Jewish background always made me measure my actions and reactions. And having pleasure always meant looking back over one's shoulder to see what wrong had been done to someone else. But if that were so, there seemed to be an imbalance. Why did we have to carry all this guilt around while others went free? I asked, "Well, how about the Stanley Kowalskis of the world? Do they have the same capacity for guilt, or are they removed from it?"

He was quick to defend his other, opposing creation, the other neighbor living in the permanent quarters upstairs in his mind, as it were. "In a sense, the Kowalskis have a great purity in that they are less divided, yuh know. They're strictly what they are. They're not ashamed of what they are. They think that's the way to be. They don't criticize their conduct very much. That doesn't mean they're bad, necessarily. I don't think of Stanley Kowalski as an evil person. I thought of him as a person of limited sensibility."

And that was it. I felt he was getting restless thinking about those two people he had talked so much about to so many interviewers over the years. Not that they themselves bored or could ever bore him. He just felt there were other people, other creations of his, worth commenting on. And so we moved on.

Tennessee's belief has often been called "personal lyricism." He said that it was as if we were each locked in a solitary cell for life and we desperately wanted to communicate. He wanted so much to do this with new works.

Nothing troubled Tennessee more than being asked constantly to comment on revivals of his acknowledged great works. The Pulitzer and other prizes were there to bear witness that here was one of the great artists of his time; it was the new works that he wished to be prodded about. After all, with each curtain on Stanley and Blanche, you somehow knew their lives would continue with new outbursts of offstage existence. But the new works were troubled and required care and love and perhaps even some charity.

Every morning from the rich "cell" of his mind would come new words and new people to populate world stages. But the critics were just on this side of hostility. Tennessee liked the thought, which

31

I put to him, that George Bernard Shaw had not written his most lasting character, Saint Joan, until his mid-sixties. And Tennessee was troubled by the precipitous arrival of *Small Craft Warnings*. In his correspondence with Billy Barnes, he expressed his unease. He wrote he was not a man who could live on prospects continually delayed. The play had opened as far off-Broadway as possible. He had objected at first to the tiny makeshift theater, reachable beyond heaped garbage and dog droppings in a part of town seldom frequented by theatergoers out for a night of make-believe. The drama was somehow too much out in the streets in those assassination-prone days of the early seventies. But Tennessee finally found some philosophical humor in the name of the theater. He said, "After some reflection—I think The Truck and Warehouse Theater has a lovely sound to it. Could it be interpreted as a metaphor for posterity?"

Like so many of his later works, the play had had its genesis in some shorter piece written earlier. In this case, it was based on "Confessional," originally published in his collection *Dragon Country* in 1969. It is about a group of life's castoffs grappling with existence and survival, searching for a kind of relief by an act of confession delivered in the setting of Monk's Place, a bar. Tennessee felt that the necessary lyricism had not made it to the stage, with some notable exceptions. One of these was the character of Quentin. He represented Tennessee's first open attempt to deal with homosexuality on stage. Quentin was almost a character in search of a more complete play. Perhaps he would eventually have found one. His soliloquy was perhaps the most poignant ever written about the despair of homosexual love, or the lack of it.

I suggested to him, "In your new play, *Small Craft Warnings*, the character of Quentin seems very important."

He was quick to respond. "He was in a way the most complex character I've drawn, I think. And I think his long speech is the best thing I've written probably in the last ten years, the best piece of writing. I thought as a piece of writing it justified the play in a way. The play, of course, is not a major work."

"But what was it that made Quentin so complex?"

Tennessee thrust his hand up to express the feeling of Quentin; perhaps he was now feeling it himself. He said, "He had been through

32

a unique crisis of self-realization which he felt, yuh know, to the point where he said it was almost like an epileptic seizure, astonishment of being himself, alive, present, in the flesh, *being!* I had felt that myself. But I was never able to express it before in my work. And I did get it through Quentin. The fact of his sexual deviation seemed relatively unimportant to me. The important part of Quentin was his capacity for astonishment in the fact of existence and his loss of that capacity. That was the important part of the speech, I thought."

"But in the end," I asked, "he still says he can be astonished, correct? Or does he say he can't?"

Tennessee said, "He doesn't say he can be. And yet I think he can be. Hah. I think the mere fact that he makes the confession is proof that he is still capable of strong emotion. Yeh."

I knew we would see *Small Craft Warnings* together in New York at a later date. I decided to touch on what was untouchable, in a way, and that was *Out Cry*, a play he hoped would be done on Broadway. Nothing he ever wrote has been more misunderstood or more meaningful to him. As time went on, I realized this. On rereading all his works and introductions, I am struck at how frequently the phrase "human outcry" is repeated. It was what he tried so painfully to communicate in so many ways.

Each day's pain has been the poetry of his writing. He said it frequently and wrote often in explanation that his greatest grief was his loneliness, a terrible loneliness that was with him day and night.

Shyness, loneliness, and fear, fear of everything, fear of just being, merged into the agony of *Out Cry*. I asked him that hot New Orleans afternoon if *Out Cry* was in fact the story of his recent life.

He said, "Yes. It's the story of the last decade, of the sixties, especially the last six or seven years of the sixties, when I was going through a terrible period of disorientation. The play is about disorientation. I believe the more popular word is *alienation* now. Although I don't quite know what alienation means. The characters are just lost, lost as I was. And the people complained and the critics complained in Chicago that it was too personal. Well, I have never valued work, created work, that was not personal. I think you have to use your life—what you yourself have experienced and felt—as the material for your creative work. Otherwise, you're just manufacturing something that is not rooted in you deeply at all. Now, *Out Cry* is not yet a finished work. It's not yet a successful work, in that I haven't fully realized its intentions and I don't know if I ever will. I'm going to continue to try to."

I could tell that just talking about *Out Cry* brought a special tension to him, and as the afternoon was wearing itself down, I thought I would move us back in time. I asked, "Going back in time, for a minute, to an earlier two-character work, *This Property Is Condemned*, the characters in it seem vital, real and personal, those two people."

He seemed relieved; he laughed. "Yes, those children. Yeh."

I asked, "Who were they in your life, those children?"

His answer was somewhat evasive. I don't know quite why. I've wondered about it often since, whether the young girl perhaps was his sister or even Hazel, his childhood sweetheart. But even now he seemed to want to keep their identities part of his own secret. He laughed again. "Oh, who were they? Well, I don't know if I want to identify them."

I tried something less personal: "But what do they represent?"

He said, "I wrote that play one night. It was the first night I arrived in New York City and I was quite lonely. I was desperately lonely and I was frightened. And for some reason I wrote that play. It just came off my fingers at the typewriter. All at one sitting. I never revised a bit of it. Yeh, it's about my childhood memories of Mississippi."

In a preface to *Sweet Bird of Youth*, Tennessee wrote that at the age of fourteen he discovered writing as a release from a world of reality in which he felt acutely uncomfortable. And there is no question that in those days in Mississippi, the Delta became a kind of personal symbol of his yearning for the "sweet bird of youth," a place of memory and inner music, before harm had come, and hurt, a period of peace and response—"You're the only star/ In my blue heaven," as Willie says and sings in *This Property is Condemned*.

The day was departing. He had been quite extraordinary in his responses. I could see, despite his enthusiasm, that he was tiring. I thought we would try one last interlude, and that was the reading of the closing passage of *The Glass Menagerie*. We moved to the balcony of his apartment, just as the piece was meant to be done on a fire escape in St. Louis. The stage direction calls for the light of the moon, but Tennessee's reading transcended the time of day or of life. He took us on the famous journey that every actor longs for, a voyage of self-discovery, time being the link between places in our lives.

And it was as if the world were lit by its own special lightning that afternoon in New Orleans. The sun was beginning to set, and a calm came over the Quarter. We folded up our tripods, cameras, and thoughts for a night of rejoicing at a day of enormous creative achievement. Tennessee let out a deep, deep sigh and said he had to "hit the sack." Victor, the always-present nonpresent secretary-companion, came out of the apartment with his portable radio tuned to the weather of the world and announced that there were tornados in Kansas, some late frost in Canada, and a minor earthquake somewhere else, and predicted an even hotter, muggier day for New Orleans tomorrow.

Tennessee raised his eyebrows in the hopes that not too much attention would be paid. And I returned to my hotel, certain that absolutely nothing now could go wrong. Like Alice, I had entered the other side of the looking glass, yuh know.

I couldn't help thinking of Blanche's observation that the human heart can never be direct. It, of necessity, must be rounded like a mountain road.

I think I was dreaming of great soft fields of cotton, or was it cotton candy, when the hammering at my door startled me the next morning. Bryan Robertson, my usually unexcitable unit manager, seemed almost toxic with shock as he thrust a copy of a wire at me. It was from the CBC head office in Toronto. It said simply, "You have not received written permission to begin filming Tennessee Williams' program. Stop!"

There are twenty-four frames per second, thirty-six feet per minute in a film. I didn't know exactly how many miles we had traveled already. But I knew, having passed through the looking glass, that stopping now would be impossible. I waved my arm at Bryan and said, "Just wire them back that it's impossible to return the images we have already captured and words recorded back to Mr. Williams. If the head office wishes to stop, let them advise Mr. Williams yesterday did not occur." (It added to the mounting sense of madness. I think if Tennessee received a telegram saying that yesterday never was, he might be relieved. Or would he?)

In the meantime, I gave the order to get the filming troops ready and said, "Let us return to the Quarter." What could they do to me, sue me?

I decided it was time to follow the tracks down the mystic road taken by that most famous streetcar, Desire. We began the day filming in the area that suggested the setting of *A Streetcar Named Desire*. Tennessee and I strolled and talked like two old Talmudic students, debating the certainty of obscurity or the other way around.

"Where are we now?" seemed like a simple question to begin the day.

He provided a verbal roadmap down the real field of fantasy. "Right now, we're on a street called Desire and we're approaching the Elysian Fields. Yeh. This is the street that goes across there, you see, and that's the street that the Kowalskis and Blanche stayed on during the course of the play of *Streetcar*!"

Tennessee talked of them as if they might just return, having moved elsewhere for a time. Perhaps they were just out of town. I asked him to, in a sense, reminisce. "What sort of family were they?"

He laughed at the memory or the question, I don't know which. "Well, it was not a typical American family, I would say. Hah. Kowalski, of course, was a Pole, and he had married this girl from a southern family which had gone to seed, like most of them do eventually, given time. Blanche, of course, was, you know, in charge of the family estate. I mean, it was left in her care and she lost it."

Of all the corners of the earth, why had he picked this corner as the house where the play was to take place?

It seemed natural as he explained it. "The Elysian Fields was the Greek name for heaven, wasn't it? And I suppose I was thinking of it ironically, yuh know. But it was anything but heaven, for Blanche at any rate."

If the street was real, more or less, how about the people? I asked, "In terms of the story, was Blanche somebody you met around here during those years?"

He insisted, "No. No. No. No."

"Does that mean you never met anybody like the Kowalskis?"

I never knew Tennessee to show prejudice against any group. He always offered a kind of courtly manner about minorities. He said, "Well, I've known a good many Poles in my life. Yes. I have known them and liked them a great deal."

I asked the inevitable question. "Do you think you are partly Blanche yourself?"

He laughed, of course, but said, "Yes, and also an equal part of Kowalski, I would guess. I've often said this—I have to identify with every character. If I'm not Blanche, I was Blanche when I was writing Blanche, yuh know. I had to be her, yuh know, at the time I was writing her to understand her."

The character of Blanche is, of course, now one of the most famous creations in all of theater. In the same way as classical actors all want to play Hamlet when young and Lear when older, all actresses when they reach an age, the bloom slightly faded, want to be Blanche. For instance, in recent times one adequate performance as Blanche turned actress Ann-Margret from a sort of delightful dumpling into a diva. The combined sexuality and frailty of Blanche have made her part of the legend of American life. She is a woman that women feel passionately about. It's been said that no playwright has ever written about women with the understanding and kindness of Tennessee.

We walked around the neighborhood to see what changes had been made in real estate since the Kowalskis left for the West End, Broadway, and Hollywood. Tennessee seemed sad that the area had not preserved its stage-set-like quality. It's hard to return to the locale of your triumph. He said, "Of course it's changed a good deal since I wrote *Streetcar* in 1947. Yeh. That building over there—that corporation building—it wasn't there. The district was all wooden houses like this one, yuh know."

There seemed little more to say about the area, real or imagined, made famous by its characters. I asked, "Why do you think that *Streetcar* caused such a deep impression in the theater world? What gave it that enormous reception it had and still has?"

We paused in front of the building where Stanley might still be aging inside. He said, "Well, I think it had very strong theatrical dynamics—two very opposite forces, the force of Blanche, which was not an unformidable force, and the force of Kowalski, which was a vulnerable force in its own way too. They were really on a collision course. One had to break, and it was Blanche."

"Is it possible to do that play and have Blanche win in the end?"

He surprised me. "It is indeed. In fact, it's possible to do it that way as they did in a Paris production. It's possible to play Blanche as a prostitute from Marseilles, yuh know. It's possible to make it very interesting that way. I loved the Paris performance."

Although it was a noisy street corner at high noon under a glaring southern sun, I asked him to do a little philosophizing, if he would, about human nature. He had attempted to place himself at one time under psychoanalysis, but he has in his own way done a better job of analyzing American society and the inner drives of man than any writer of his time. I asked him, "Do you think the forces that Blanche and Stanley represent are forces that exist in every person?"

"Yeh. They are there within each person. In the play they are opponents, but they are the two sides of every human nature. And, of course, Blanche makes her most important speech when she says that it's important to people that they develop certain little areas of sensibility. She doesn't say it that way, yuh know, that's the meaning."

The speech he referred to was, of course, the magnificent soliloquy by Blanche. It is in a way the anthem of Tennessee. In it he cries out, through her being and voice, that we humans are a long way from being created in God's image, but that there must be hope because there has been some progress in music and poetry and human tenderness. It is Tennessee's plea to humanity to give love and tenderness a chance. It is his desire to pull us out of our own angry darkness, to make us more than animals. It was the speech, not by accident, given to the increasingly "mad" Blanche.

"That was the jist of what she says. Yeh. But my sympathy was quite divided. Hah. Although I'm not for brute force. No. But I think Stanley was defending what he believed was his. Yeh."

(The transcript notes "wild talking," and I'm not surprised.)

*   *   *

New Orleans meant freedom for him. When he left what he called "dreaded St. Louis" as a young man, it was like moving from the darkness of black and white to Technicolor. I heard him call St. Louis "St. Pollution," and even now when they say he has "been laid to rest" there, I say, "Not likely," which is perhaps why his restless ghost is even now glancing over my shoulder and his laughter and lamentation are inside my head.

It had been tough going for him financially when he started in New Orleans, but his creative spirit soared. In a short story called "The Angel in the Alcove," his powers of romantic description eclipsed themselves.

He talked of the city and the moon being like sisters, which is a great romantic image, the image of young longing. He says of them that they have learned to understand each other and speak to each other in a wordless way, as two sisters aging gracefully together. He credits the fatal attraction of the moon for bringing him back over and over again as it did to the city where he first found real love. It was the place he found solace when he was so often savaged by critics. But in the early days, of course, before he knew success, he found New Orleans a sympathetic haven, a refuge from the failure he felt. Every man must find his own Jerusalem for his own inner spiritual peace where he can find comfort just in being in a local atmosphere out of harm's way. He felt New Orleans deeply.

That May noon in New Orleans, we walked along the streets of memory. The garlic and jazz saxophone sounds drifted from alleys. Each doorway held the faint flavor of nostalgia. I have on my wall now a faded photo of him in that time, outside a door numbered 722, his profile stamped on it like an old Roman coin.

Now it was time to explore the bohemia. "This street," I asked, "I think it has a particular meaning in your life?"

"Yeh, this is the first place I lived for any length of time in New Orleans. This house, number 722. It was a rooming house at that time. Right now it seems to be unoccupied and locked up. But it was a very colorful place."

It was, in fact, the place where hunger helped bring on images of the angel in the alcove. I said, "You had a little less money then than you have now."

"Oh yes. I worked for the landlady for my room and board.

The room is that attic up there with two gable windows. Hah. Let me read you the start of that story. It catches the flavor of the time, yuh know."

And so he read with delicious delight of himself so long ago.

He told me of that first landlady of his. He claimed that suspicion seemed to be part of her nature and that this had left him with a vague sense of guilt. Although his famous landlady had her own room, she chose to sleep on an uncomfortable cot in the hallway, so none of her lodgers would be able to enter or exit without being observed. She would shout "Who?" if anyone passed in the night. He made his exit by way of a couple of sheets bound into a night rope.

But it was her ghostly shape in the unlighted hallway and her constant scrutiny of night visitors that stayed in his memory. It seemed to appeal to the Puritan in him, being able to pass the guard of the night, his own angel in the alcove. It was the tingle of young sin.

It was the challenge of minor mischief.

He finished telling the story by almost licking his lips and then let out one of his punctuating laughs. He admitted freely that he enjoyed reading his works and seeing them performed. I think he quite enjoyed putting his old landlady in her place in his writing, the lady who called "Who?"

I asked him to think back, to remember what New Orleans had meant to him coming from St. Louis.

"Oh, it was my first contact with a free society, I mean a bohemian world, yuh know, which I really encountered with a bang here. Hah."

I asked, "Was it an encounter that involved blacks and whites together?"

"Oh, well, yes. That difference didn't affect my life very much."

"Some of the people who have written about you said that you've come from the 'Sad Soil of America.' "

He denied the notion. So many "scholars" have tried to dissect Tennessee's world. So many have become tangled in prejudices. So many have latched on to a cliché of him and his terrain. And even after being dismissed by the man themselves, they hang on, leech-

Holly and Adam Rasky play the parts of Tennessee and his sister Rose during the happy years of his childhood as Tennessee reads his poem over the nostalgic setting.

Adam and Holly Rasky as young Tom and sister Rose. She dances on the edge of the sea. The poem tells of her voyage into early madness.

Young Tom Williams is left behind by his sister who disappears into madness. Adam Rasky takes a fall and is yet to forgive his father, the director, Harry Rasky, for not stopping the cameras as he cries over his wounded knee.

Actress Carol Williard as Laura in a scene from The Glass Menagerie, *filmed in a cramped room at the Algonquin in New York.*

The Gentleman Caller is Michael York in The Glass Menagerie.

The always marvelous Maureen Stapleton, one of Tennessee's favorite actresses, plays Amanda, patterned after Tennessee's real life mother, Edwina.

The Gentleman Caller, Michael York, announces he must leave to pick up his girlfriend.

The shattering news of a girlfriend is received by Amanda who tries not to show her open disappointment.

The confrontation between Amanda and Tom, played by Jim Naughton. Laura listens in terror, ready to return to her world of the glass menagerie.

Tom shares with the audience the start of his career of wandering. The scene will dissolve to Tennessee reciting the soliloquy from The Glass Menagerie *in New Orleans.*

Proud of his reading from Out Cry, *Tennessee announces to Rasky and the audience that there certainly should be a ''Bravo'' now. And there is.*

like, to academize the artistic, which is impossible. Art just is. He said, "I don't know what they're talking about. I don't feel any particular sadness in New Orleans, do you? In fact, I feel just the opposite. I think the people here are life-loving people."

"How about earlier on, Mississippi and Tennessee. Were they sad places in your early childhood?"

He denied this as well. "I wouldn't specify any single part of America as being the sad soil, yuh know, unless perhaps some of the underprivileged areas of New York City or some of the other big cities. Yeh."

"So the South is not sad?"

"I don't find it sad. I'm sure there is misery in the South as there is everywhere. But it doesn't represent sadness. Romanticism, yes, romantic melancholy, yes. But although I suffered a great deal of privation here—I used to have to go and bum a cigarette, yuh know—in the morning. Still, I was not sad at that. Life is too full of adventure, yuh know, and change."

You could see around the streets the parade marching by, a kind of swagger and beat of rhythms. New Orleans is its own kind of soothing song. You could almost dance to it.

He was, as Gore Vidal pointed out, a great complainer. But he was also full of the joy of life, longing to taste every experience.

No man baptized by the bawdy flow of chicken blood and anointed by the rain of chicken feathers can ever be indifferent to the killing colors of life.

After our walk through the French Quarter, we sat at a sidewalk café to continue the exchange of life stories. We found we shared a common bond—chicken plucking. In my case, I came by it through inheritance, my father having been a *shoichet*, a ritual slaughterer of poultry. I would work through the long, cold Canadian winter nights, witnessing the deaths of thousands of chickens on their way to kosher dinners, plucking the lice-filled feathers one by one, like endless grains of sands of the sea. Tennessee listed it as one of his "survival professions" while waiting in the wings for success. Out in California he worked plucking squab and dropping feathers in a milk bottle for each animal so defeathered. This, along with being an usher at the Strand Cinema in New York and an elevator operator at the now-departed San Jacinto Hotel, constituted his *Nave Nave Mahana* season, the title Gauguin gave his favorite Tahitian-era painting, meaning "The Careless Days."

This was much different from his potential ritual death at the shoe factory in St. Louis that meant sameness, boredom, and depression from debasement of the human spirit. He was surrounded by other young men also searching for the rainbow of creative acclaim. He wrote of that time, "We were continually sailing our small crafts, each with his crew of one, himself that crew and its captain. We were sailing along in our separate small crafts, but were in sight of each other and sometimes in touch, I mean huddling in the same inlet of the rocky, storm-ridden shoreline and this gave us a warm sense of community. . . . To have a problem in common is much like love and that kind of love was often the bread that we broke among us. And some of us survived and some of us didn't and it was sometimes a matter of what's called luck and sometimes a matter of having or not having the gift to endure and the will to." At any rate, he had endured what Moss Hart once described, in verbal color-painting, as "the brown taste of poverty." He had endured it and never forgot it.

In his recollection of that time, he said, "When I was one of the young and gifted, and living among others of that kind, there was no self-pity among us, at least no degree of it that distinguished us from the rest of humankind."

No matter what temporary work he had to do, he always considered himself a poet or writer. He wrote his first play in his grandparents' home in Memphis in 1934. It had a title of longing: *Cairo! Shanghai! Bombay!* and was produced with local success at the Rose Arbor Little Theater by an amateur group calling itself the Memphis Garden Players. But all those exotic places in the title were not as far from Memphis as Broadway.

As we sat and ordered a bottle of red wine at that sun-drenched café in New Orleans in May, I asked, "Coming from St. Louis to this street as you did, in those early days, did you say to yourself, this is where I'm really going to be a writer?"

"Of course I'd been writing for a long time. Oh, yes. But I think I matured somewhat as a writer here. I became a mature writer only after I came to New Orleans."

"Why was that?"

He leaned on his elbow in a characteristic pose, questioning me and himself at the same time. "The city had a liberating effect upon me. My whole personality felt free. It gave me an inner security I didn't have before. I was able to write better. I began to write with maturity. Probably, I think, most of my early work was not ready, more or less junk. Hah. I began to do some good stories in New Orleans and some reasonably good poetry."

One of these poems was called "Lament for the Moths." The Professor had alerted me about it and recommended I pursue this theme, a recurring Williams symbol, the moth. And now he read the poem for my film, one of several. His purring southern sound gave wonderful rhyme to his words, so that a line such as "Lament for the velvety moths, for the moths were lovely" made you see these powdery moonlit creatures in flight before your very eyes.

I recalled his stage direction description of Blanche in *A Streetcar Named Desire* suggested a moth avoiding a powerful light.

So when the reading was over, I asked, "In a way, Blanche was a moth, right?"

"A very strong moth. Sort of a tiger moth." And he laughed.

Since most of us, I think, would be more drawn to butterflies, say, than moths, I asked, "Why do you have this feeling about moths? Perhaps obsession. What is the fascination of the moths?"

"It represents to me," he said with some seriousness, "delicacy. Vulnerability. Delicacy."

"But hitting the light—" I said.

He interrupted, "That's what destroys, yuh know. Strong light."

I kept on the theme. "But they say that moths also have this tendency to want to destroy themselves. I don't know if it's true or not."

He laughed at the idea. "I've never seen them do that. But I have seen lamps, outdoor lamps, in places like Mexico where you see all kinds of night creatures; I wouldn't say necessarily moths that incinerate themselves on the hot panes of the lamps, yuh know."

I asked him to expand a little deeper. "In a way, the aging actresses in your plays are kind of moth figures, too, are they not?"

He replied quickly, "Oh yeh. I think my concept of these 'vulnerable' people has undergone an evolution in my work. I'm be-

43

ginning to recognize more strength in them than I did originally. I see them as being stronger now."

He had another glass of wine, enjoying himself and the afternoon wine. In my time with him, I always felt he had a very low threshold for alcohol consumption. A half-bottle of wine was enough to make lines slur and cause his complexion to redden. He reluctantly read another poem called "Mornings on Bourbon Street" from his volume *In the Winter of Cities*. He called it overly romantic.

Once again I thought it best to turn to more recent works and the present day. I suggested he might like to read something from *Small Craft Warnings*.

He seemed not quite happy with the work, not yet. He said, "Well, I'm still working on *Small Craft Warnings*. I'm thinking of changing the title to *The Living Quarters Above*."

He confessed that he was a peculiar blend of the pragmatist and the romanticist and even the "crocodile." He said that he had to be all those heroines and all those heavies.

Small Craft Warnings is a play in which all the many parts of him are in a constant state of confession.

Obviously the character of Doc, whom he felt he resembled, and his grief concerning age and accomplishment were something Tennessee wanted to try to debate by way of the play. I asked, "In that play, you say we are all winners and losers. How do you rate yourself now, at this stage of your life?"

He said, quietly and thoughtfully, "I think we're all winners and losers in rotation, yuh know. We go through periods of winning and periods of losing. I've gone through a long period of losing, a good ten years of it. It's a bad, a hard habit to break. And when you've had ten years of it—well, I'm not as optimistic about my new work as I was. I don't think I'm about to turn into a big winner. But I still enjoy my work, even when other people don't enjoy it."

It is impossible to assess how much of what he said he truly meant. Tennessee loved challenging people with broad statements to get a reflective reaction. He'd gotten in the habit. He said that he hammed it up in interviews and became purposely outrageous to become "good copy." He gave as his reason a need to let the world know he still existed.

44

Existence itself is one of the major themes of *Small Craft Warnings*. Tennessee read Doc describing ("in a voice filtered through booze") the character Violet, one of the small craft drifting on stage. She is described as being not quite there. The word he used was amorphous, something or somebody suggested instead of complete.

It was this question of "amorphous" that I wanted to explore. I asked him, "Are we all amorphous?"

His answer was complex because the idea is complex, I suppose. He said, "Well, no. In the production of *Cat on a Hot Tin Roof*, I said that my purpose as a writer was to catch the exact quality of life. Not through naturalism. You can't catch the exact quality of life in naturalism. I think that a person, any human being, is always, like a cloud in a way, being blown, yuh know, being blown around through a continual metamorphistic changes in form. But that is not the same as amorphous. Only a few people are really amorphous in the sense that the character of Violet is amorphous. Most people have form—I would say that you, Harry, are a man who is fairly well, yuh know, the opposite of amorphous. Hah."

I still don't know if that was a compliment or not. We'll see.

I wanted to go a little further into the *Small Craft Warnings* characters because the play was so much on his mind. I asked him to talk about Quentin, the eloquent homosexual.

"I would say that Quentin was a man of great possibilities who had settled for something far beneath his potential in life. To me, he seems a person of stature, at least potential stature, because his speech is the speech of a very cultivated mind. I therefore felt that Quentin was a truly tragic figure. I could have written a whole play about Quentin and perhaps should have. But I didn't."

"Is that you, once again—are you Quentin?"

He would not settle for the simple question, and by now I should have known better. "A lot of it is me, just as a lot of the character of Leona is me. The only character that I truly identified with was Steve. You remember Steve? Hah! I could completely identify with him. He was contenting himself with the scraps of the world, one of which is Violet. You know, he says, like a bone thrown to a dog. Yah."

I don't know how much was now serious and how much was

the heat of spring. He meant it. He didn't mean it. Both were correct. Take your choice. The wine was flowing. So I thought I would have another try at the question of the South.

He said, "I have said many things about the South. Yes. The South is a country of my past as well as my birth. If I were writing about Yankees, I promise you that I would find every bit as much damnation among Yankees and maybe not as much charm. I don't think of my people as little people. Not as long as they keep qualities of courage and gallantry. Those are important qualities, and I think of them as southern qualities, very much. I think they're bred in the bones of the people I wrote about, such as Amanda Wingfield and even that little girl in *This Property is Condemned*. I write out of love for the South really, but I can't expect all southerners to realize that my writing about them is an expression of love. It is out of regret for a South that no longer fully exists. My childhood was spent in the South, and childhood is always a magic part of life. In the South there may be a greater sense of honor and decency and of tradition, which I don't think the North ever had. And there's less of the dog-eat-dog attitude, perhaps. Though it disturbs me, of course, to find the South becoming, at least that part which is apparent on the surface, so conservative in its social point of view. But I think back of this facade of conservatism, there is a great deal of wildness in the South."

After this subconsciously lengthy analysis, there followed a brief and extraordinary interchange, totally spontaneous. After all, it had been a rather heady couple of days that were now drawing to a close; the conversation and wine had flowed and the temperature, I think, had affected both equally. But the interchange has become the most quoted part of the finished film (frequently through unauthorized use in somber biographical compendiums).

I began by asking him, "Do you think the wildness is still here?"

"Oh, very much, yeh. The private lives of people here are infinitely wilder than they appear to be on the surface, yuh know, in the open."

I asked then, "Is that indeed why there's so much wildness in the characters of the plays you've written about the South?"

Getting into the rhythm, as it were, he paced his answer. "Yeh,

I like to show the surface of their lives and to show what's back of the surface, yuh know. It makes an interesting contrast."

So then I asked what I thought was the next obvious question. "Do you think that's why people everywhere can relate to your characters no matter where they come from?"

He responded with some enthusiasm. "I think of myself as a very, very eccentric person, and I don't see, yuh know, how the majority of people could relate at all to the people I create. Don't you think?"

I suggested, "Perhaps it's the eccentric in each individual they see—in themselves, in a more hidden way."

Now there was the greatest outburst of almost frantic laughter. For the first time in the laid-back, easy-striding atmosphere of the sunny street in New Orleans, people stopped to stare as the man in the vanilla-white suit and red kerchief let out a howl and rolled back his head and raised his glass to toast the camera—the world. He cackled, "That's a relief to hear that. It's very encouraging. I shall now continue with my eccentricity."

Let it be noted that the transcript of that day now lists "wild sound on the street." I would not quarrel with that.

I suggested we make it a "wrap," the end of this episode of filming. As tired as he was, he said, "No. One more poem. I want to throw one more poem at you, called 'Shadow Wood.' It was used for a play I wrote called *The Milk Train Doesn't Stop Here Anymore.*"

And so he read this poem with great fire and tender feeling. I didn't know at the time why, but now I think I know. It ends with a plea for tenderness. Why, he asks, is it so hard for "shadow man" to say tender words? Why indeed!

Somewhere, I think, in *Out Cry*, the character in search of himself says he never knew there were so many boundaries to cross. Yes. We had crossed a boundary, he and I, or "I and Thou," as Martin Buber said, along the line where the imaginary streetcar rides to Desire and beyond to the Elysian Fields, where people can know each other in a way that few of us ever come to know another soul, to become in Browning's phrase "a soul of my soul." I believe I let out a giant sigh that afternoon in Tennessee Williams' South.

47

I asked if he would autograph a volume of his plays that I planned to read on the plane on my way back to Canada. He said, "Why do that now, Harry? There will be lots of time for that. We can meet in a week or so in New York and keep at it. This is just the beginning."

"Who knows what will happen between now and then?" I suggested.

There was the usual laugh. "Have it your way, Harry."

And so he inscribed the book, now in front of me, "In case of crash, fondly, Tennessee Williams."

Amorphous no more.

It helps to be sure of yourself in planning a film. Talent, too, is essential. But neither is of any use without luck. When I arrived back in Toronto from my adventure in New Orleans with my treasure of film, I knew I had something quite wonderful in the making. But there was that small problem of having begun an enterprise costing several hundred thousand dollars without the necessary bureaucratic signatures. My natural enemies, paradoxically, came in to save the day. A German television company, Polytel, had offered some advance money as coproducer for the German-language rights, so I was grateful for the kindness of strange people. And the Shell Oil Company's International Division was looking for a way to spend money to set themselves up not as price-gougers but as patrons of the arts—and they promised to be gentlemen callers of the most discreet kind.

It is one of those curiosities of history that no approval was ever officially given. But on the other hand, I was not stopped. This kind of "stage life" haunted the film until its completion. And by the way, it is still going on. A film is never finished as long as new audiences are interested in it. The film changes, depending on the level of appreciation of the moment.

I found myself back in New York being greeted by the friendly doorman of the Elysée Hotel. "Your brother's right inside, Mr. Williams' brother."

As the days went on, I stopped protesting this familial link and probably even sounded more southern. This was a Tuesday, and Tennessee insisted that that was the best day for a lunch because that's when they served stuffed peppers, which were, he insisted, my favorite. I never found out why he made this assumption. So it was stuffed peppers and a bottle of Soave, his favorite Italian wine, followed by "dry tea." He always ordered dry tea, and sometimes it came without clarification. He assumed that any civilized place would know that it meant the tea bag on the side. And I have been ordering my tea that way ever since: "Dry tea, please"—the drink of the poet.

Tennessee was prone to patterns. Lunch was always at noon, after he awoke from his morning nap, after having spent a couple of hours at his typewriter. Dinner always followed viewing Walter Cronkite and the news; it never came before. He usually had steak. Come to think of it, I don't know if he ever did order the stuffed peppers for himself. It was my favorite, he insisted.

Staying at the Elysée Hotel seemed to be a kind of dedication to those ghosts who haunted its corridors. Of these, he loved to talk of the fabled Tallulah Bankhead. He was to refer to her as "a tramp in the elegant sense," and he said she knew no shame. He seemed to admire her skill of continuing a conversation that started in the living room and went on nonstop into the bathroom while she relieved herself, with the visitor being invited to come right in while all this was going on.

His favorite set of rooms was the "Victorian Suite," with a separate area for the companion-secretary of the moment. The rooms were tiny, with paint that always seemed about to flake and what seemed like velvet upholstery, more memory than style, almost as if there were a hope that time would stop in the corridors outside, too confused to catch up with the transient resident. But stage settings such as these could only temporarily prevent the inevitable.

Our lunches had a comic matinee quality about them. The discussions usually were light, touching on family affairs: "Mother is not well again"; "Dakin is running for office"; "Sister Rose is smoking too many cigarettes." Sometimes they concerned Tennessee's health: which new doctor had given him which conflicting advice. His preoccupation with his health was obsessive. What was there to say to a man who in 1946, at the moment when he first found his theatrical pot of gold, had debated whether to bother buying a new suit, as he was sure he would not live long enough to wear it? Perhaps it is true that we begin dying the day we are born. Most of us don't actively concern ourselves with that, except in moments of physical stress or during the closing years. But for Tennessee, he seemed aware of it every day. Dying was a full-time activity some days.

At the Elysée that day, after the dry tea had been consumed, he decided not to visit a doctor but suggested I come along to see the production of *Small Craft Warnings*, now transferred to the New Theatre uptown. The leading lady now was a transvestite named Candy Darling. As the years have passed, I have thought many times that Tennessee's decline, if that can be judged, began with the casting of this strange creature in his work. Up until that time, his works, although they bordered on the bizarre at times, had always been redeemed by the dignity with which they had been presented, as well as by their obvious poetic power. But the production of *Small Craft Warnings* was now taking on the character of a circus. Tennessee was determined to keep it alive for six months so that his beloved *Out Cry* would be easier to mount later on as a commercially viable experience. So not only was Candy Darling now flaunting herself on stage, but, some weeks later, this would be followed by Tennessee himself acting onstage as the character Doc, followed by postproduction seminars. Somehow, some border line had been crossed, and taste had been tossed into the nonexistent balcony.

That merry matinee, I sat with him in one of the back rows as the curtain was raised and Violet began a singing mumble of "The Wheel of fortune / Keeps turning around."

Tennessee began a loud laugh that echoed around and he continued almost nonstop. The woman in front turned angrily and said, "I am trying to enjoy this play, would you please stop laughing?"

Tennessee laughed even louder and responded, "If I can't enjoy this play, who can? I did write it!"

The woman scowled at him, not knowing whether to ask for an autograph or for her money back. There's no question, and I saw it later on in other productions, that what sometimes struck Tennessee as funny in his own works was a puzzle to others. I don't know if he was laughing at his words, or at a botched performance, or at some secret he had worked into the script, or perhaps at the events that were leading to his death. I don't know.

Even those who knew him best and longest seemed baffled by

Tennessee Williams on his balcony at New Orleans. He recites from his classic work The Glass Menagerie.

Tennessee outside the building where he began writing in New Orleans. He recalls that he was so poor he had to bum a cigarette from his landlady. But those were happy days, before fame came his way.

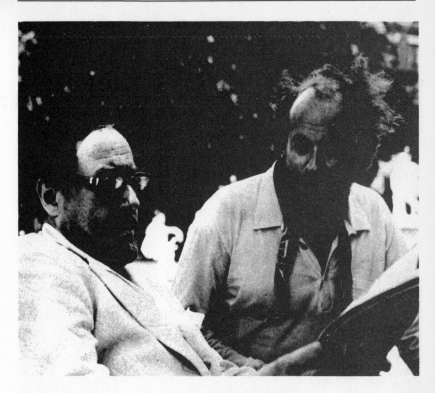

Tennessee and Rasky at lunch.

Tennessee was a reluctant fisherman. This day he was haunted by his past.

The rectory in Columbus, Mississippi, where Tennessee was born.

Williams and Rasky in the park in New Orleans where filming began.

A house like this in "the Elysian Fields" is where Stanley and Stella lived and where Blanche came to call.

John Colicos and Colleen Dewhurst discussing a scene from The Night of the Iguana. *The actors' natural discomfort increased the drama.*

John Colicos seemed to be standing on the edge of the earth.

Our film crew in search of Tennessee's past on the Mississippi borders.

his characteristic of launching into semihysterical laughter when no one else quite knew why. The Professor, Oliver Evans, now taking his long-awaited, last, lingering look at the Orient, at our expense, wrote me from Pattaya Beach:

Tennessee, for as long as I've known him, has always been able to laugh, and quite sincerely, at things I never thought even remotely funny. And the remoter they seemed (from what I thought was funny), the harder he'd laugh. He'd laugh at an incident at which most people would even be tempted to cry and this used to be one of the many things I never understood about him. Also, he disliked people intensely who took themselves too seriously; this has continued right down into the present. He himself has a horror of being confused with people of this type, of having it ever said of himself. And so he has deliberately set himself the task of playing the clown where an attitude of solemnity or reverence would normally be indicated. He is terribly afraid of being thought insincere, or pompous. I've often thought he forced himself to laugh out of fear of being thought maudlin or sentimental. As you well know, one of the classical charges against the romantic is that they lacked a sense of humour and especially that they were unable to laugh at themselves. I can think of no one else since Shakespeare who has woven humorous scenes so successfully into plots which are basically tragic, or, to speak more precisely, pathetic.

The play over, the matinee of laughter and lamentation over, Tennessee said, "I think it's time for you to meet sister Rose, Harry."

I said in mine heart, Go to now. I will prove thee with mirth, therefore enjoy pleasure: and, behold, this also is vanity. I said of laughter, It is mad: and of mirth, what doeth it.

Eccles. 2:1–2

Just as Siamese twins may be joined at the hip or breastbone, Tennessee was joined to his sister, Rose, by the heart. The blending of the two souls was so complete that they could have occupied a single body. In the history of love, there has seldom been such devotion as that which Tennessee tenderly showed his lobotomized older sister.

51

Much has been written and analyzed about their relationship. In this area, I think, amateur analysts must beware. It was more complex and fragile than any of us can know or understand. But I do know and at the time became instantly aware that no film on Tennessee, no examination of serious intent, could be complete without at least wishing to understand the bond that tied them closer than any umbilical cord. There is Rose in everything that was Tennessee. Even now, I can feel her stare, a look so penetrating because it would not turn away from shame or embarrassment, those artificial niceties that had been surgically eliminated so long ago.

Miss Rose was the victim of early lobotomy, an operation performed in the sadistic days when psychiatrists thought a scalpel could solve problems of the emotions, an operation approved by his parents. It brought, of course, a kind of partial death. Rose, who had been inseparable from Tennessee, outgoing and full of life, may well have needed treatment, but the operation that took away part of her reasoning left an open scar on Tennessee. There have been various versions of the story: the mercurial moods, the too-ripe sexuality, the mother blaming the unloving father. But Tennessee was away at college at the time, enjoying one of his periods of rest from environmental trauma. Maybe he blamed himself for not being there, for not preventing the butchery of rational thought. Perhaps the guilt haunted him. What is certain is that Rose was there everywhere with him, no matter where he was, as if he were a man trapped in a room of too-scented flowers.

He had suggested that the dinner meeting with Rose take place at the Plaza's Oak Room. And I knew that the invitation was meant for me to see and understand many things that were necessary if I was to understand him. How can you respond to an invitation that carries as its subtext, *Come view my pain. R.S.V.P.?*

Rose came south from Stoney Lodge in Ossining, where she lived in a room with "flowered wallpaper," where she stared with eyes that seemed to see the flowers grow. She arrived by limousine at the Plaza Hotel.

How perfectly the poet had caught the feeling in "The Beanstalk Country."

He had written of that special, direct way that the mad enter a room, their eyes full of wild zones we never dare to cross.

And so Rose entered, from space we could never enter. Tennessee gallantly took her arm as if he were escorting her to the ballroom dance floor, and led her to our special table by the window, introducing her to my wife, Arlene, and then to me. Her comment was simply, "Yes." It represented I don't know what.

And so we all examined the menus. And Tennessee said to her, "I think you might like the chicken, Rose. I know you like the chicken." He was mother-father-brother.

And Rose said, "Chicken. Yes, chicken."

And so she stared at us with eyes that never looked away, looking at, looking at, looking for, staring, yes. . . .

I tried, I suppose, to join in the conversation, and my wife, so lovely a soul, passed the rolls and kindness as if Rose had been in our world that day.

"Chicken today. Chicken tomorrow. Chicken. Yes. Chicken." She rhymed like a participant at Alice's mad tea party.

And Tennessee looked at me with a shrug as if to say, "Now, Harry, hear me. Now see my life. Now see my love." But he only laughed that lost laugh of his.

Rose waved to imaginary people out the window and urged us all to join in waving at her friends in the misty New York night who could not be seen by those who knew not where to find them. Tennessee said later that once Rose claimed she was waving because she was the Queen of England. I don't know. But she had some world we did not see in which she was in charge.

At one point she got up, presumably to go to the ladies' room. Arlene followed or led. "Washroom. Yes. Washroom." Some minutes later, they reappeared, Arlene, looking as kindly elegant as always but now a little shaken. She reported that Rose had entered all the stalls and flushed all the toilets and returned.

So here he was, master-supreme of words, talker and teller of ideas complex, with his beloved, who talked one word at a time in one-word sentences. And how was one to respond? *R.S.V.P.* There was a strong, overpowering scent of roses in the air. I think, even now, even now, I smell that scent.

Yes, it is the scent of The Beanstalk Country.

And some small person came to fetch Rose. And Tennessee

walked her gently down the long marbled corridor of the Plaza and took her to the limousine, paid for by *Summer and Smoke* residuals. They walked like a couple in a glass bubble that you shake and the snow begins and a nursery rhyme spills out its repeating childhood theme, a childhood never ended.

What was he seeing? I suppose a long-ago beauty made of glass.

We left the hotel together, Tennessee and Arlene and I, silently, but not with any spoken despair. The caller had come and gone and we had mutually experienced what he had experienced every day after the scalpel took reason and the sister he loved, and still loved, with it. We offered to drop him at the Elysée on the way down to our apartment at Waverly Place.

"No," he said, "let me out at a corner."

"Which corner?" I asked.

"A corner," he repeated.

I think maybe it was Second Avenue and Fifty-fifth Street. I don't know what was there, if anything. I don't know what was going on in his "leftover heart" that night. There was a terrible "hot" silence between us, if that is possible. The shared experience of the first dinner with Rose was impossible to follow with small talk or perhaps even large talk. It was as if one were watching the outcome of a great love drama in which one of the pair does not die but is forced to carry with him or her the other person living in body but only in half-mind. What love couple of history could have survived it? Tennessee did, or partially did.

Out into the dark, siren-filled New York night. To where? A long walk along mugger-filled streets? Cruising? The search for the empty companionship that increased the terror of loneliness that eventually had to be smudged out for the night with sleeping potions?

"Chicken. Yes. Chicken. Flush. Flush."

So I held the hand of my wife Arlene more closely. We were together. Children were waiting. We had a living history of companionship, with more to come. Oh, I think I felt more wont to express my own outcry to my new friend but could not that night.

54

But little words of tenderness
are hard for shadow man to say.

I suppose I knew even then that a certain bonding was necessary if the film was to have any dimension beyond the ordinary, a bonding not only of ideas but of brotherhood. There was a need to actually splice our families together. A film can only produce passion in the viewer if the passion has been felt, studied, and reworked by the filmmaker. No matter what the subject, the subject must also be the filmmaker.

The very first visual material I attempted was to put to film the words of his gentle poem "Paper Lantern," an ode to the sister who left him behind, that begins with a line about the race through life's emotions. She was always quicker than he was.

Here was the sister first leaving him behind in skill and then "vanishing" into madness, going faster and further than he could ever go in an escape from the reality of the pain of life. I decided to use my own children, Holly and Adam, as visual symbols for Rose and him. I dressed them in the pastel calico patterns of the past. We started with a brief sequence shot at the Stratford, Ontario, Shakespearean Festival grounds, where they tried to outrace each other on antique swings with horses' heads. And then later the sequence would be concluded at Key West, where Holly sat trance-like on the rocks of the Atlantic and then began a slow-motion dash with Adam. They were the same age difference as Tennessee and Rose: she was six or seven and he four—no match. As they approached the camera, running in their children's marathon, Adam tumbled over, his shoe flying in the air, his knee scraped, and he began to cry. His father, the director, allowed the camera to continue rolling while his son, the actor, wept. Adam has never forgiven me to this day, when he sees the film, for not coming to his rescue. But the sequence was the perfect setting for the words of the sister who could not, would not, stop for a racing, loving brother stumbling behind in pain, as later narrated by Tennessee and set to memory music.

And images of poems danced through my head. I made an early decision not to use existing film material of Tennessee's work because the rights were so complex, and also I wanted to try my hand at interpreting this man who had now dug so deeply into my being.

The first dramatic segment would be a recent piece, since it was very much on my mind: the speech of Quentin in *Small Craft Warnings*. Although the play is set in a bar, "a place of refuge for vulnerable human vessels," I found in Stratford a gallery with modern paintings that seemed to have in their disjointed images the stresses and strains of the quality of the soliloquy. The choice was reinforced because one of the paintings contained the image of a giant phosphorescent fish, and the speech began with talk of waking one night and finding a giant fish swimming over the character's head and the quality of surprise it would evoke or not. I asked William Hutt, a leading Canadian Shakespearean actor, to play the role of Quentin. Aside from the then-current off-Broadway production, he would be the only one to have attempted it. He seemed perfect for the part, with a quality of sophisticated boredom. His delivery had a certain painful sting, like tooth decay. The colors of the paintings seemed to float with the words, like the sound of a sad saxophone. It was a most eloquent human cry for help, a voice wanting to be young again, to believe again; to be surprised by the world, please.

I make a challenge here to those who continue to say that Tennessee wrote nothing of consequence in those later years. My challenge is simply this: Of any play written in English since that time let him who criticizes find a passage as perceptive and poetic as the long speech of Quentin. I say also that for homosexuals there has never been an aria with so much lyrical heart as this statement by Tennessee. Here is the glaring intensity of a soul pleading for understanding.

Quentin tells it as it is. He insists that the thing that you must never lose is the capacity for surprise. He says that even if awakened from a deep sleep he would not be surprised to find a giant fish sailing above his head.

Tennessee, through Quentin, blames part of the pain of awareness that he has lost his capacity to be excited again by life on the harshness of the homosexual experience, its predictability. He compares it to addiction of a needle by an addict.

He is not kind in his honesty here.

He tells of remembering when it was all so different, so fresh, so alive, so full of surprise. In fact he is almost religious in his adulation and adoration of the life force.

He talks of the explosion of embracing the lightning of life.

I know of no greater passage in literature stating man's simple appreciation of existence.

As the summer proceeded, mail continued to arrive from exotic outposts from my correspondent-at-large, Oliver Evans, who was carrying a suitcase full of Tennessee Williams literature through the way stations of the Orient. From Singapore came a note:

> I'm wondering if in your documentary you are planning to stress the fact that in so much of Williams' work the prevailing pattern turns out to be the gradual, but systematic and inevitable disintegration of a person who originally was in some way distinguished—a definitely superior individual in short. Indeed, so much is this the case that the title of one of his minor works, "Chronicle of a Demise," might also serve as a motto for the major body of his productions. The characters are usually women, but sometimes, as in the case of Reverend Shannon, they are men.

The letter went on at some length and closed with:

> I do want to earn my money, like an honest whore . . . return address . . . "Tourist Mail" . . . c/o American Embassy, Wireless Road, Bangkok, Thailand.

I wish that I had had the funds to fly my crew to some exotic place like "Wireless Road, Bangkok" to film the scene from *The Night of the Iguana*. I wanted to try to capture the Reverend Shannon and his loss of grace, his search for God. It struck me then, and still does, that Tennessee was a profoundly religious person, and even though he could not follow the given traditions, he was constantly agonizing over God's seemingly casual attitude toward pained poets and those who were guided by their supersensitive natures. (What did God have in mind?)

I found in the brilliant and brooding Canadian actor John Colicos, I thought, the perfect person to play the part. He seemed to contain desperate anger. I decided that he needed a powerful leading lady to give the scene its great dimension, someone like the calm earth with the potential fury of the sea. I decided to go after Colleen Dewhurst. Anyone who could have survived two stormy marriages to George C. Scott had to be able to tame the spirit of Tennessee's fallen priest. I discovered, through her helpful New York agent, that she was spending the summer vacationing on Block Island with her children.

I made one of those spontaneous decisions that are only possible in the documentary situation: Go where the action is! I offered to move my small film crew to Block Island and take John Colicos with me. This, I think, surprised everyone. But why not?

The island had exactly the quality that I was after in my mind's camera vision. I wanted to see this setting as a place that could have been the edge of the earth, a place beyond which there could be no further retreat for the priest, running and hiding from his past and the inner devils trying to devour him. We combed the island for perfect settings and, as I had rather expected, ended up on the front porch of Colleen's cabin. It was, of course, neither the Mexico of the movie nor the design of the play, but the feeling that you could at any moment drop off a cliff into eternity was totally correct. We were aided by awful weather, so that a mist seemed to devour everything, and the constant pulse of the warning signal from the island lighthouse alerted all small craft to beware of storms to come.

There was enormous unease between Colleen and John Colicos, but their personal distance enhanced the production. As the stage direction says, in the time Reverend Shannon confronts Hannah Jelkes in *The Night of the Iguana*, they are like two actors in a play which is about to close on the road, preparing seriously for a performance which may be their last one. It was an agonizing afternoon. The desperation of Shannon and the cold surface of Hannah were quite magnificent in this duet, acted out at the edge of the earth among the tall grasses leaning anxiously in the salt wind.

So perfect, it seemed to me, were the words written by Tennessee that any variation was easily detectable. If either John or Colleen forgot a line, the entire rhythm was suddenly lost. The poetry of the passion had to be exact.

There was also something about the tough beauty of the vegetation that caught my eye. And so we filmed struggling sunflowers and lonely wild roses fighting for life in the sand, which later I would use to help unravel my story, married to the words of the ancient poet of *The Night of the Iguana*. The poem is a plea for courage to take hold of the frightened spirit.

Those dwellings of his golden childhood would be my next locale.

For Tennessee, before bewilderment there was the South of ease and peace.

Later in his complex, hazy novel, *Moise and the World of Reason*, he would write of approaching darkness in a room where all that he would hear were the footsteps of the great being, as quiet as they were large, footsteps of the Great Unknown One approaching our world of reason or lack of reason.

And not so far back, in *The Night of the Iguana*, Hannah cries out that she was one of those people who could be young without really having her youth, and not to have her youth when she was young she found truly disturbing. But her work was her therapy. She was lucky.

Tennessee *had* to work in the same way to find courage, to overcome fear. He had gone from the childish sunflower joy of his grandparents' warmth to the grimy cruelty of industrial St. Louis and a savage world where surgeons severed nerves under the banners of healers of mental disturbances. Before the dark storms of youth, there had been the lovely light of those rainbow days "with frames of colored beads in Kindy Garden."

I went with my camera crew to Tennessee and Mississippi in search of those comfortable joyous mornings, but they proved to be as elusive as silvery soap bubbles as I tried to find "where did he come from—where did he go?"

In an enthusiastic moment in either New Orleans or New York, he had said that he would join the camera crew and me as we made our pilgrimage through his past. So it was no wonder that in the state of Tennessee, as a result of our advance bookings, we were greeted outside the Ramada Inn by a huge marquee that spelled out WELCOME DAVID BOWEN CONGRESSIONAL NOMINEE AND TENNESSEE WIL-

LIAMS. I don't know what happened to Mr. Bowen, but Tennessee was not part of the group with the film crew.

The sign did have one favorable result. Along the main highways I had not been able to find the kind of scenery I imagined would have been part of his early days. But a young college student came to the motel looking for an autograph. He was certain that I was Tennessee, attempting a northern accent. When I convinced him I was not, I explained that we needed a suitable setting for the film because our guide, Tennessee, had not arrived. I suppose I knew he never would, but I like dreams like that. The young man and his girlfriend said that his own parents still owned a small plantation of the kind I described. And so we followed him for miles, down back roads and dirt roads, to a place not known on any map, and there among the miles of cotton fields and the coccoonlike growth of Spanish moss winding around and around the trees and the earth, I found the most unreal settings that seemed just right. We trained our cameras on black shacks and the lonely simplicity of the past-tense-looking South that even then seemed imagined. I was trying to film memory.

In Columbus, Mississippi, I filmed the rectory where Tennessee was born and had little trouble finding the actual birth record, still there, written in clear ink. And then on to Clarksdale, the "Blue Mountain" of his plays. It is a quiet city of two rivers, the Mississippi and the Sunflower. He remembered it with descriptive fondness in "The Resemblance Between a Violin Case and a Coffin."

Perhaps the single most powerful visual shot taken on that adventure was a picture of a lone black boy striding up a copper-colored dirt road, the Mississippi dust flying about him in his dance-walk, and all around him the silence of the acres of cotton. It would become part of the title sequence in the finished film. You could conjure up any place and time, cozy and distant. Tennessee wrote about the safety he felt listening to his black nurse, Ozzie, tell tales of animals that had human traits. And where was Ozzie now? That black mother-figure who served as a substitute for the mother-of-record, the woman born with high heels, Edwina, waiting for the last waltz of fading beauty. (As Tennessee said, "Home is where you hang your childhood.")

There were still those about, old-timers, who remembered the

Williams clan. One old redneck leaned over tall hedges and said, "I don't reckon young Tom should have used that family of his to write about. Those are family secrets." (Then what else is literature?)

I found quaint St. George's Church in Clarksdale, where his grandfather had served as rector. And just in time, just in time. The wrecking ball was about to smash through its stained-glass windows, destroying the fighting and innocent saints of old.

Time haunted him. In *Sweet Bird of Youth*, how often he repeats the theme that an almost silent clock is merely readying for a dramatic eruption that will destroy the world we know. There is no way to cheat time.

I came to Key West with my weather report of time, the slow decay and erosion of the visible monuments of his past. Tennessee was waiting for me, both anxious and apprehensive. No one had ever quite tried to follow in his footsteps, to record the settings of his childhood. He wanted to hear, but somehow not too much. We slipped right back into the formal but relaxed filmed conversation.

I was impressed with the distance south I had had to come. Was he retreating further and further from memory? I asked, "You travel back to the most southerly point in the United States. You seem to want to go south, south, south, south all the time. Why is that?"

We were sitting in the courtyard of his garden, at the simple house at 1431 Duncan Street. It was humid, with no breeze on the pink oleander blossoms. He said, "Well, you know that I am devoted to tropical climates because I can swim all year round.

"I came here originally in January of 1941, when the third Mrs. Hemingway, I think it was the third—Pauline Pfeiffer Hemingway—was alive, yuh know. Came here in 1941, and I took a little cabin for seven dollars a week in back of the biggest house in Key West. It was called 'Tradewinds.' I began rewriting *Battle of Angels* there. I went there on the hundred dollars I had received from the Theater Guild. Of course the money ran out very fast, even in those days. But I was delighted with the society down here then. It was really pleasant, great. Yuh know, there weren't so many hotels, and it was really primitive in those days. It was simple, like a frontier town."

The conversation began in this simple, nostalgic way. It was

61

then that he told me that he had begun work on his memoirs. I think this was possibly inspired by the fact that he was telling the outline of his life to my camera, and he thought he would fill in the details in book form. When the book, *Memoirs*, did finally emerge— and it took another three years—it would turn out to be a strange amalgam of sexual confessions and deep inner study. But it was a formless and strangely unbalanced book, one he later confessed to me "should never have been written and never published." I was told he wove into the original version the setting of our film confessional, but it was later edited out, as was the introduction that he had suggested: "You just might want to hear. I'm sorry if this looks like two Manhattan telephone directories."

And so he continued:

Well, here is the beginning. As I was saying to you, not all of this should be taken quite literally because my moods change, and this is written as sort of a day-by-day thing, yuh know. When I began this thing—this chapter is called "To Begin With," and it happened this morning—I was in a very angry mood I think, over having to write my memoirs. But I'd received a fifty-thousand-dollar advance to write it, and I couldn't turn it back, yuh know. So I had to go ahead, and I was angry mostly about that. And so he read a long passage from his *Memoirs* about being a very angry old man. He said that he considered anger as a very important emotion, almost cleansing in its power. It seemed to me that he was very much like the Preacher in Ecclesiastes who fears the world that will come after him. The passage in the Bible and his own reading were almost identical. The Bible says: "Yea, I hated all my labour which I had taken under the sun: because I should leave it unto the man that shall be after me. And who knoweth whether he shall be a wise man or a fool?"

Tennessee wanted his readers to know that he was disappointed in them, that he had tried to understand and love them, but felt that was now impossible. The anger of the day made him feel that he should take all his works and his own body and have them dumped overboard in a clean white sack. He was drastic, all right.

He requested that when he die he be buried at sea. He wanted his body dumped over at a point near where Hart Crane drowned. He said exactly that he wanted to have his body returned to the sea from where all life originated.

He seemed to be picking up the tone of his preaching grandfather. He was like Jeremiah in Lamentation calling out, "Is it nothing to you, all ye that pass by? behold and see if there be any sorrow like unto my sorrow."

Having concluded his overture of sorrow, he broke his stern expression and said to me, "I'm sure that will do."

So this memoir was to begin in anger, anger later deleted by an enthusiastic editor, perhaps, but here confessed to my camera and sound. He felt forsaken. As always, at that point where the truth is most painful, the record shows "wild sound of laughter."

Why so wild then? Was this his morning joke on the world? The beginning of the memoir disappeared, never to find its way into print. The will that he so clearly defined to me apparently did not in its last version have this sentimental request for his burial at sea. I don't know. So much is unknown, and that is why I think that any attempt to launch biographies that claim to be accurate can only catch the darkest side of the elegant moth that was Tennessee Williams. He had to be seen in flight. The moth in repose is an enormously inelegant and uninteresting creature. It is a brooding puff of powder. In the air, it defies our imagination; its mystery is magnificent.

At the moment I thought I would follow the Hart Crane clue, the writer who seemed to have been so powerful an influence. I recalled that in *The Night of the Iguana* there is a line that says someone couldn't paint Hart Crane because there was so much suffering in his eyes.

Tennessee said, "Yeh, they couldn't paint him with his eyes open. The Mexican painter Siqueiros said he couldn't paint him with his eyes open, he said, because there was too much suffering in them."

I asked, "Thinking of that play, I wonder whether the priest, Shannon, and Hart Crane had certain similarities?"

"I think so, don't you? Except they had opposite sexual bents." He then let out one of those truth-laughs, if that is what they can be called; the painful laughter of his truth. "His life seemed true.

He could not have a deep sexual attachment to a woman, yuh know."

I don't know of whom he spoke exactly here—Shannon, the agonized priest; Hart Crane, the suffering poet; or Tennessee Williams, the pained and giving playwright. Or maybe all three?

Since I was determined not to have the interview break down into a quiz game about sexual deviation and of questions to which no answer was possible, I allowed our conversation to dwell again on the question of his theology. I said, "The character of Shannon fascinated me so much because of his concept of God. Is that your own?"

He seemed to appreciate the thoughtfulness of the direction of the conversation. He answered with some seriousness. "Not precisely. I don't—I can't—I cannot in any way that is plausible to me explain my feeling of a personal God, if that is the term you would use. That is, a God with feelings for, who is capable of feelings for, the individual. And yet I know I do pray. I've made a lifelong habit of prayer. And I've always had the sense, however mistaken it may have been, that I've had either affirmative or negative answers."

This seemed to be enough for him on this inner theme that day. He broke the mood of devout contemplation with his little joke of the day. He said, "Hah, that brings us to the title of Truman Capote's next book, doesn't it? *Answered Prayers*. A beautiful title. Hah!"

And again the mad laughter of relief. In the time I knew him, there were many references to Truman. Each man seemed to respect the suffering of the other. They admired each other's skills. Truman made a point of publicly joking on talk shows about Tennessee's lack of knowledge of current affairs. Tennessee mocked Truman by merely raising his voice an octave or two to capture the boyish quality of literate outrage. But they cared deeply about each other, each understanding the other's agony over the assaults of the world on the other, dedicating books to each other. They were brothers of a raw, sensitive kind.

It was deceptively calm that day in his garden as we spoke of his memoirs and God. The sun played in and out of the branches. Perhaps I should have taken as a kind of warning the comment of

Vee in *Orpheus Descending*. She says that all our lives are mixtures of light and dark, and that mixture complicates life. I was dwelling on the light, not realizing what shadow I could bring. I said, "Sitting here at Key West, thinking of you contemplating your end, I've just come from Dixie, Mississippi, and seen the beginning. Could you describe Columbus? I know you were very young and small, and I know you were back there once. What was Columbus, Mississippi?"

And so he wove the fabric of his thoughts into the past—what I thought would be only the pleasant past. He said, "Columbus, Mississippi—well, all those little towns in Mississippi where I lived with my grandparents were very happy. They made a very happy background for my childhood, yuh know, for my sister's and my childhood. And Columbus, I must have left at the age of two. I have very distinct memories of that."

I tried to conjure up the geography of the place for him. I said, "Going through Mississippi with my film crew, I was impressed with the 'sea of cotton.' Almost like snow, everywhere."

He liked the image. "Oh yes. The cotton was in bloom, was it? In full bloom—I don't know what you say—the cotton is high."

I asked, "Do you remember from your early days the sight of cotton?"

He was going back in his mind with me, along those copper, dusty roads of time. "Yes, indeed, very very clearly, and the gins and the cotton gins in action, and all that. When we were going to do the *Battle of Angels*, Margaret Webster, the English director, told me she had never seen the South. So we flew down from New York to Clarksdale, to Memphis, rather, and it was the first time I had been on an airplane. No, the second time. And we had to put down in Nashville on account of thunderstorms. We were sent to a hotel, but they woke us about an hour after we had gone to bed and said the storm had passed. And we went back to the plane and continued down. So we spent maybe twenty-four hours in Clarksdale, and she said she saw the South. Hah. She was now ready to direct the play. Hah. Which may have had something to do with its misfortune, I think."

Of course, the early production of *Battle of Angels* was his first major disappointment in the theater, and hard to forget.

Now I made a painful error. I started to tell him about the destruction of his grandfather's church. I asked if he remembered the church in Clarksdale.

He said, "Yes. But I don't recall the name of the church. I do remember the church."

I told him it was St. George's and that the wreckers were already tearing it down. It was like a jab, the surgical removal of a childhood time that had seemed permanently set in time and space. Smashed bricks, cracked windows, eliminated ancestors. Much of it must have struck him, as he grew silent for a moment and then went on.

"St. George's. Yes. Yes. The one in Canton was called the Grace Church. The one in Nashville was called the Advent, Church of the Advent. The one in Columbus is called what? . . . I don't know."

I told him it was St. Paul's. "But in Nashville that church was very close to a place called the Centennial Park. Your mother recalls in her book you playing in Centennial Park."

His mother sent him to the park with the servant. She said, "For a while I thought Tom would end by talking like Ozzie, who spoke with a plantation dialect."

Now time had been displaced. Memories flooded through. He seemed to be there, in the past. He spoke with his unique plantation sound. "I remember playing in a park. I remember picking wild-flowers in a park, and I remember kindergarten—a sort of experimental kindergarten in Nashville. And I was very delighted with the alphabet blocks and all that sort of paraphernalia—the color crayons and everything. Mother slipped out of the room. And when I discovered she was gone, I started to howl and stomp on the floor, and I made such a racket that she heard me all the way down the block and had to come back and said it was the end of my kindergarten career."

Back, back in time. I wanted the memories to be as visual and as particular as possible. Maybe it is a kind of hypnosis, I don't know. But I was trying to guide him by the hand so he would step in the same footsteps he took as a child, to walk along that child's path.

I suggested, "Along the banks of the river, I imagine sometimes you would run and play with your sister?"

"You're talking about the Sunflower River. Well, actually, no.

66

Rose, I, we never played along the banks of the Sunflower. At Clarksdale, the school that we went to was across a wooden bridge on the other side of the Sunflower River. But sometimes the school-children would take a walk with the teacher along the banks of the Sunflower River. I remember seeing a black baptismal service occurring, a Baptist baptismal service in the Sunflower, yuh know. And the blacks were all wading out into this river in white shifts, yuh know, and it was quite beautiful."

Deeper, deeper, closer, closer to that time. Softly, I said, "There was a feeling of adventure when you and your sister played."

He was fully there, in the magenta mood of his own history. "Well, sister and I were unusually—my sister and I were unusually close as children, I think mainly because at the age of seven I had this very, very, very bad case of diphtheria, which made me virtually an invalid. I think my mother made me feel more of an invalid than I actually was. She put such emphasis on my weakness—she even claimed I couldn't walk. She talked me out of walking, I think, for about a year. So I was naturally thrown mostly with my sister as a companion. And so my sister and I grew so used to being company for each other that we tended to rely on each other's companionship rather than seeking friends, yuh know, outside the household."

That skipping music of memory seemed to play inside him now. They were arm in arm, in games of childhood. I whispered, almost: "As a child, was Rose very outgoing, lively—?"

He now interrupted, wanting to make it quite clear, no mistake must be made. "Much more. Much more. There was no trace of her later schizophrenia. She was very imaginative and lively."

"And I suppose as you played she might stop and see something on the ground—an animal or something, and comment—"

Again he stopped me to go on with his revelations. "Oh yes. She was much quicker. I wrote a poem which I think I will read for you. It begins: 'My sister was quicker at everything than I.' It appears in *In the Winter of Cities* in the section called 'Hoofprints of a Little Horse.' "

And so he read this quiet elegy to that time and that sister who skipped right past him and no longer waited for him but who fell terribly into madness, leaving him behind as she roamed the other side of the looking glass of the mind. He dared not follow, and the separation was a brutal cut that could never be healed. Now there was none of the agonized laughter. There was an intense seriousness to everything.

I said, "You've been asked this question so often about *The Glass Menagerie:* Does Rose haunt your work?"

"Oh yes. Yes. Yes. In fact, all three of the three or four of them, my female relatives, are very much in my work, the ones connected with my early years in the South. My sister Rose, my mother, my grandmother, for whom Rose was named, and Isabel, my father's younger sister. They were all interwoven into my picture of southern ladies."

His mother wrote, "I always thought of Tom as a small pitcher with big ears; he would sit perfectly quiet, never saying a word, listening with every sinew." He claimed he visited dying parishioners with his grandfather. She said, "To Tom, as to all children, seeing an adult die would have been a fearful experience."

I thought it best now to come back to the present. I could see the past shadows crossing his eyes in a way. I wanted to pull him out of that darkness. "But here we are, and you are writing your newest play, *Out Cry*, about a brother and sister again."

"Yes," he quickly corrected me, "but it has no relation really to *The Glass Menagerie*. In fact, when I was trying it out this summer, or the summer before last, in Chicago, an earlier version of it, and I went on a TV program and the moderator had interspersed the interview with me and members of the cast with clips from that awful film they made of *Glass Menagerie*, and I flew into a terrible rage. . . . Hah. . . . And it was successful because he eliminated the whole film clip. I didn't want that there be any inference to similarities between the brother and sister in *Out Cry* and those in *Glass Menagerie*."

The mood was now different. I asked, "Who, then, are the people in *Out Cry*?"

He surprised me. He said, "I think they are two sides of one person. Really. Some student made that comment when the play was performed—when the play was read, rather—at Purdue University last winter."

I asked him now to read the opening monologue, which I then admired and now still admire. Before doing so, he offered this preface: "Yeh, this really is a one-character play. Well, at the beginning the brother is setting the stage for a performance which they are to give in some very faraway primitive theater. They cross many frontiers. He remarks at one point, 'I didn't know there were so many frontiers in the world.' Hah. They've arrived at this final theater, and the play opens."

And so he read that to play with fear is like playing with fire. There would never be a reading like it. The text was butchered between his reading and the Broadway presentation. Sad to lose such language. When the monologue was finished, he smiled as if coming back from a long, pained journey. He laughed again. "There should be a bravo now."

Yes. Yes.

If only there had been a way of salvaging the rich tone of his feeling about that work. You could feel the vast loneliness, trapped in a Mississippi world without hills or mountains, no way to find a horizon, only vast fields of copper-clay flatness, eternal flatness without perspective.

"Take care of me. I'm frightened, don't know the next step!"

The phrases of *Out Cry* were his very real plea. It was the terror inside himself that he wanted us to hear. Perhaps it was too great for any theater. That Key West morning, I switched the conversation, perhaps because of my own inability to suffer with his suffering. There was the usual self-embarrassed laugh, and we continued. I asked, "You seem to have this preoccupation about going alone to die. [How true it turned out, how true.] You know, one thing that struck me in New Orleans is that the whites are buried above the ground and the blacks are buried below the ground."

He was surprised. "Is that true? How horrible!"

I asked why he thought that was so in New Orleans.

So we had a brief clinical conversation about burials. He said, "I suppose they bury people above the ground in New Orleans because the city is beneath sea level. You see, then the water would immediately seep into the coffin. I thought everyone there was buried in stone crypts."

I repeated again that in the black cemetery we visited, the people were buried below the ground. He was troubled by this. I suggested to him that the blacks seemed so much a part of him.

He responded with a thoughtful nod. "Well, Harry, I think whatever indigenous culture America has produced has come from the blacks. Our music, our humor mostly, our dancing. The great body of our entertainment seems to me to have a black origin. I think that ultimately when the two races, the white and the black, when their blood is mingled, through the passage of time as has already been accomplished to some extent, I think it would produce the handsomest race on earth, and perhaps the strongest."

I reported on the swing through the South to him and on what I had seen and on what we had in fact filmed. "In Mississippi I noticed some of those old shacks are still there on those great plantations. Did you as a child see that sort of squalor in the back fields?"

"No. No. Not very much," he said. "Not very much squalor. We noticed, I suppose, those little cabins on the edge of the cotton field. And I remember Mother reading to us about a Christmas night in the black cotton pickers' quarters. It was written by a poet from around Mississippi. I don't recall his name."

"But would you have played with black children?" I asked.

"No. We didn't mingle. But we were forbidden by our parents and grandparents from ever using terms of denigration about blacks. We never did."

I suggested to him, "But there was this distance between the cotton fields and where you were, I suppose."

He responded, "There was no mingling, not in my time, as there is now. Not long ago, I flew down from St. Louis to New Orleans with a young black man who was head of a theater down there, and he said to me, 'I wonder why we're talking so easily together?' And I answered him, 'Because I always felt I was black.' "

"And what did he say to that?"

"Well, he laughed. He drove me to my apartment. I entertained him at dinner, and we're still friends."

At this point we all seemed to be wearing a little thin. Tennessee suggested that he would like to break for lunch and have a swim. There also seemed to be some increasing discomfort as the hours passed. Columbus, Canton, Clarksdale—all those places seemed to be unwinding inside him. Robert Carroll, his young man of the moment, indicated that lunch was ready. Robert was a short, well-built blond person in his mid-twenties. He had been through Vietnam and seemed to like to spend the afternoons in a cloud of smoke. Some of Tennessee's close friends found him difficult; I had no problem with him. But he did always seem somber. There was little light at the end of his tunnel.

During the lunch pause, we filmed the grounds and the studio in particular. I had wanted to film him swimming, but he resented the idea. He seemed suddenly shy. So we stopped. He seemed to be increasingly irritated. After lunch, a breeze was shuffling through the vegetation. He appeared in a checkered silk bathrobe. It was a kind of coquettish challenge. I think this was to show he could be somewhat outrageous. I thought it best to begin the afternoon with uncomplicated questions.

I asked, "I think it would be interesting to know a little bit about an average day in your life, if there is such a thing. When you're here, where do you write and how long and that sort of thing?"

He obliged politely. "Oh, I write in there, in the studio there. I've turned over the back room to Robert. He writes in there. Well, I've always written in there since I built the studio around the early fifties. It was the first thing I built here, before the pool or anything."

I wanted to know how long he wrote every day.

"Well, it depends," he told me. "Some days I write six hours, and some days—I don't think I wrote more than an hour and a half this morning."

I suggested, "Which is probably why you're a little depressed."

"Yes," he laughed, and let it go at that.

His answers seemed disconnected. "It's a very isolated kind of place," I said, pointing around to the garden on what seemed like an obscure street, in the most southerly part of America on that hot, late afternoon. "The characters in your plays are real, very real, or seem to be very real. Do they just float around in your mind?"

Out Cry was never far from his mind, as was obvious with his answer. He said, "The characters have to have reality for me. I think the problem is to make them real to other people. As the work becomes more personal, I think it becomes more of a problem, yuh know. To make characters that a large audience can identify with, I think it's going to take all the skill of the director, Peter Glenville, and actors Cara Duff-MacCormick and Michael York to make that

71

happen with *Out Cry* because that's really such an interior sort of play."

He seemed well aware that *Out Cry*, which would have its try on Broadway before my film was finished, was a turning point of his existence at this stage of his life. It is, in my own estimation, despite critical destruction, one of his great works. It is his most highly considered later piece of work. What it lacked then and still does to this day is a great production that understands the poetry and translates it into action. The actors would have to suffer and soar, and the director would have to have the most intricate control. (I wouldn't mind trying to direct it myself someday, just to see if he was as right as I believe he was. Give this piece a chance!)

Being such a bird in flight, I wondered if the travel interfered with his work.

He said, "I travel a great deal and it doesn't stop me from working."

I developed this funny notion that he would have to reserve a large number of airline seats to move around, to have all his characters-in-creation make the trip as well. Or would they develop different accents as he moved from South to North?

He assured me, "Oh yes, the characters aren't affected by changes of location."

We took a pause while he read for me his poem "Mornings on Bourbon Street." He said it was "dreadful." Not quite. The work perhaps of a young writer trying to find his poetic sound, but it has a few lovely lines. It is extremely nostalgic and concludes with the poet weeping.

Remembrance always seemed to start an inner weeping.

A change of mood seemed necessary. I thought he might talk a little about humor. In one of his lengthy footnotes to our history, Oliver Evans, my traveling adviser, had written me, "As for humor in the plays generally, though there is a great deal scattered throughout most of them—most of the important ones, that is—I can think of none in which it is central to the main action. It is—more often than not, *black humor*, if you know what I mean—and I'm sure you do. The kind that lies close to tears, and it's usually rather grim—But perhaps I'm too finicky. And maybe too academic as well, for I've just finished reading Aristotle on the subject of comedy, and was impressed by what he said, to the effect that the truly comic automatically excludes that which is painful."

And so I said to Tennessee, as he sat dressed in his oriental checkered robe looking like a diva who had just left her bath, "Humor is very important in your work. I know you must have some funny work you can read."

It was an occasion for a howl. "Yes, becoming funnier. Hah."

"Why do you say that?" I asked somewhat incredulously.

"Because I'm working mostly with funny subjects."

I regret that I did not follow this with a probing question. He was in a strange seriocomic mood. He wanted to show a more campy side, if that is the word for it. He read for my camera the delightful poem "Life Story." It begins telling of two people who meet and go to bed together without knowing anything of each other's story.

It goes on to tell of the increased boredom of the two strangers on a bed that leads to exhausted sleep with a lighted cigarette, concluding that that's how people are incinerated in hotel rooms. I think he was trying to shock me a bit. (The poem is always a show-stopper at screenings of my films, read as it is by him with a kind of catty, naughty delight.)

Everything seemed so good-natured. I pressed him to read one more poem, and it was, I suppose, a poem too far, as it were. The band of memory was pulled beyond its normal strain. He read "The Beanstalk Country" and explained how he came to write it.

His tone hardened. "Well, of course, we used to every Sunday—we were living in St. Louis—and my sister had just been committed to the state asylum in Farmington. We used to drive over there, yuh know, and she would receive us in the sun room, the solarium, yuh know, and it was intended to give you a very cheerful aspect on the place, which was, of course, a very horrible one, . . . if you looked behind other walls."

And so he read about how the mad made their explosive entrances.

Disturbed. He had become disturbed. I could see a fierceness in his eyes. But I continued on, following the ghost. "Do you think this haunted thing you have of your sister is ever going to end for you?"

73

It was an impossible question, and the answer was naturally evasive. He said, "Oh no, because one of the things I most enjoy when I go to New York is having her come in town, yuh know. And having dinner at the Plaza. She's very funny at the Plaza, yuh know. She's been cut down to three cigarettes a day, but as soon as she's seated at a special table in the corner, she will say to Miss Josephine Healey, yuh know, her companion, she will say, 'Excuse me, I have to go to the dressing or ladies room,' and she'll get up and . . . she'll go straight to the cigarette counter and buy a pack of cigarettes. And she'll open them right in front of Jo. So defiantly it's done. Blowing this puffing smoke at her—"

I interrupted to say, "You have a great fondness—"

But he wanted to make the most important point of all. He stared deeply and perhaps angrily, I don't know. He said, "And so we have a great relationship. I mean, her condition hasn't—doesn't terminate our contact, yuh know . . . our feeling for each other at all!"

I think that was it, the key to it all.

How we feel about each other, how we love each other, how we need each other—all were embraced in his continuing regard and love for Rose. Madness and surgery of the mind should not end passions, he was saying. Do we stop loving an amputated person? How can we still call ourselves brothers to man or woman? In *Out Cry*, the sister cries out, "Oh, what a long, long way we've traveled together, too long for separation. Yes, all the way back to the sunflowers and soap bubbles, and there's no turning back."

No turning back.

I suppose I didn't then know how to handle this natural, painful, complex revelation. My record shows I tripped off into points made before. "In the end, I know you want to have your ashes thrown to the wind, and so on. Do you want to be remembered?"

He repeated, "I don't think it's going to make much difference to me."

He had begun to show deep fatigue. I gave the direction to the crew and said to him, "Okay, I think we can cut it. Okay. I think that's all we should do today. You've been a good subject so far. Does it sound like a good thing to do tomorrow—to go in a boat?"

He said quietly, "I think it would be lovely."

I gave instructions to Bryan, my unit manager. "Okay, we'll book it. We'll book a boat."

He seemed agreeable. Tennessee said, "Yuh know, I haven't been on a boat this time, or this trip."

A voyage at sea. It would be relaxing. What could be more serene?

The morning after. The morning after the long day of discussing and reading and laughter, I greeted Tennessee, who was in the only dark mood I ever knew of him. As we picked him up to take him to the waiting boat, he was almost sullen. He said that he had had a night of nightmares. He saw all those places of his childhood in vivid pictures in his dreams. He had seen his grandparents on slabs in a mortuary that was the decaying church in Mississippi. His blessed Grand and the real Nonno had been disturbed. He had not slept well. He had tossed and turned and could not find solace. He had had cold nocturnal visitations. He was tense and, I think, resentful at having to go out to sea, but remained polite even if it was a distant feeling. I had inadvertently stepped on the grave of his sacred past. The child who did not want to look on the dead was disturbed.

And so we left to go deep-sea fishing, a detached playwright, an all-Canadian film crew, and a director looking for direction. In a sense, I suppose, our small craft became a ship of fools. When a conversation is called for and one of the parties decides to be silent, it can be more disappointing than fishing with no sign of a fish. There is something quite ridiculous about bait dangling off a line at the end of a luxury boat when the fish have unanimously decided to look the other way. And so this journey in the coastal waters would prove almost futile, since Tennessee closed up, like an oyster hiding his secret, rich pearl. His night of pain would not go away, despite the sun. It was the only day of discomfort I ever knew with him in ten years of association. I suppose that it is true, as Tom says in *The Glass Menagerie,* that time connects the landmarks of our lives, and the voyage of discovery that I had vicariously taken for him had profoundly disturbed the order of his existence, and the night of nightmares that followed would now, inevitably, in its way, cancel the day.

I tried to go around the dark mood. A fishing pole was incongruously thrust into Tennessee's hands as he looked somberly out to sea. I said with artificial good nature, "I wanted to ask you, during this so-called masculine atmosphere, about your father. What do you think of him now?"

He stared at seagulls trailing in the ship's wake. He said, "I feel a great deal of affection for him now. I think he had a tragic life, yuh know. I don't think it was as bad after he separated from the family as it was during the time he was with us. I hope it wasn't. Any man who starts to drink that heavily must be unhappy, yuh know?"

I offered, trying to fish for thoughts, "Trying to say something."

Tennessee said only, "Yes," and watched the birds caught by the wind, flying sideways with difficulty.

How often does the bird appear in his works? Yes, we were chasing the elusive bird of time and hope.

That day at sea he was totally sympathetic to his father, who long ago fell in love with long distance. This was in total conflict with the version of his life expressed by Edwina in her book *Remember Me to Tom*. In it she is constantly nagging away at Cornelius, her ill-suited and long-departed mate.

Oliver Evans had recommended to me that I read a short play called *The Last of My Solid Gold Watches*, in which a character like Big Daddy appears. He is, coincidentally, also similar to Arthur Miller's Willy Loman in *Death of a Salesman*.

I asked, "To what extent is the character in *The Last of My Solid Gold Watches* like your father?"

He said, "Yes, he talked very much like my father, and so did Big Daddy. They spoke more or less the same vernacular."

I tried to ease into the conversation. "But in *The Last of My Solid Gold Watches*, I wonder to what degree the sort of decay of that man as he was looking for the roads he used to know is the story of the South. Is it a kind of parable?"

"Yes, I suppose," he said, trying to be agreeable, I think. But then he questioned the answer, "I don't think I was thinking of any conscious parallel. It could be taken that way. I don't know if the South has decayed. I suppose industrially it's on an upward grade, isn't it? But I suppose the days of the great plantations are over."

I asked, "How about southern society?"

He offered, "Southern society has undergone a great transformation, I should think. Yeh."

I tried to get him to expand. I said, "Mr. Charlie talks about the good old days and how he can't find his way."

"About the roads, yeh. I believe they don't even have traveling salesmen anymore, do they? I'm not sure. I suppose they have Fuller Brush men, that sort of thing."

The answers were going nowhere. He had become a reluctant subject. And when I look now at the photograph taken that day, of Tennessee looking troubled, neat and tidy in a sort of gray lounge suit with a mess of suntan lotion splattered across his forehead, he looks like a night owl forced out into the sun, a moth in search of cozy darkness. I'm surprised he didn't try to throw me overboard as bait for the nonbiting fish of the too-early, too-bright, too-forced morning.

So I tried this: "There seems to be a kind of poetic relationship between the Big Daddy character, Mr. Charlie, and the old black man that he encounters."

His answer: "Yeh."

I tried again: "Mutual comprehension?"

The answer: "Yes. Yeh!"

"Is that kind of, in a way, a symbol of the black, the old South— the black and white not understanding each other?"

Answer: "Yeh. Yeh."

Question: "And a kind of respect for each other, perhaps? Is that true? In a strange relationship?"

The diary of the day notes "a long pause." I'm not surprised. When the questions become longer and more complicated than the answers, it is time to quit.

Fortunately, a fish came along. Not a very big one.

Tennessee said, "That bird is after the fish."

I think the bird won.

Anything seemed in order in the awkward way of things. I suggested, "Do you think that people are like birds sometimes? People sometimes compare birds to people." (Gore Vidal always seemed to refer to Tennessee as "Bird.")

He said, "I often have flying dreams. I think people love flying. I would like to fly."

Small talk would not lead to big talk. That was certain. I tried going back to the plays. "Are Mr. Charlie and Big Daddy—are they at different stages of a person's life, would you say?"

His response was not considered. He said, "They're both close to the end of their lives, aren't they? Yes, Big Daddy and Mr. Charlie."

Neither the fish nor the playwright were biting. I thought perhaps I would try his own expert on him. "Oliver Evans says you seem to have a love for seeing human beings who have nearly reached the end of their rope, and they want to try for something greater. Do you believe that this is a major theme of your work?"

Tennessee was having none of this theory, although he continued with strained politeness. He said, "I don't think of it that way, although it may be so. Oliver teaches my plays, yuh know, and probably he has examined them critically more than I have, perhaps. I don't think that theme would interest me so persistently, yuh know."

So I decided Oliver could not come to our rescue, lost at sea. I said, "Big Daddy seems to have a kind of optimism about him, even if he—"

Tennessee interjected, "Yes. Yeh."

"That was obviously purposeful, I suppose."

Answer: "Yeh."

Question: "Did you see your father that way?"

And so he gave his last answer of any reasonable length. "My father was very vigorous. Yes. A very vigorous man. And very life-loving. Although maybe that's not the right word, *life-loving*. When I say that he was unhappy, I think he liked and even loved the life of the road, and he was very disappointed when he had a desk job, yuh know. He was disappointed when he was tied down with the family to a desk job. I think his only escape was in the bars and in the poker games, yuh know. And maybe the weekends at a little country club."

I asked, "Do you sort of think of yourself as being on the road, with the amount of shuffling around you do, Key West today, New York tomorrow, and so on?"

"Practically, when seen that way." He offered a slight laugh. "Yes, I don't stay long in one place. No."

Still constantly searching for the *bon mot* of the day, I said, "So in a way, you're a kind of traveling salesman of plays. Or life, or what?"

Answer: "I think I'm just restless."

Question: "Why?"

Answer: "I don't know why. My father was, and I am too."

And that was that. I instructed the captain of our disappointed crew to head for home, fishless and almost interviewless. The sun was now out of Tennessee's eyes. His tension eased a little. I asked if he found the sea especially relaxing.

"I like the sea. Yes. I love long ocean voyages. I was distressed to see the President Lines have been discontinued. Oliver and I, yuh know, we crossed on a President Lines, the *President Cleveland*, when we went to the Orient last."

I asked him, as a last question on the boat, if he would take a long voyage on a ship again.

"No," he said. "I'm too restless now. I want to be where I am going, yuh know, quickly now."

On the way in, while the line dropped suddenly, it suddenly whistled. There was a bite and a modest spurt of action as a bonita caught hold.

He smiled for a moment. I said, "If only the critics could see you now."

He managed a final, weak laugh. "They'd be scared."

And then there was silence for the rest of the short, long voyage home. The restless spirit wanted off the small craft. He wanted an end to it.

It was agreed that we would meet again in the afternoon on dry land.

Before lunch I sent Bryan over to his house from our motel with two airline tickets I had promised. He reported back a scene of anger, tickets and curses flying in the air. I never witnessed any scene such as this. But Bryan reported to me that it was awful. He was shaken.

There are grave robbers, and I suppose I had become a memory robber. Tennessee just could not function that day. When we arrived at his home after lunch, there was a note pinned to his door, scribbled by him. I have it now, the ink faded brown, fading like the photograph on my wall.

Dear Harry—
the old man is
finished till 4:30. . . .
The rum-coco and the
wine did him in.
His apparition will
return for a session
at above-mentioned
time. I want to
borrow that shirt
that says "Shitty
Day"—it could
explain a lot. Love 10.

He was referring to Bryan's T-shirt that had emblazoned on it the campy greeting, "Have a shitty day." Nothing went unnoticed or unused by Tennessee.

At four-thirty we returned again. This time Robert Carroll came out of the darkened house. He was like a messenger from the battlefield. Tennessee was still sleeping and would not be able to see us. Could we try again in the morning? I explained that it is difficult to keep a film crew sitting around, especially on a limited documentary-size budget. But he was the messenger, not the decider, of the day.

I made a decision that seems to occur in every film of this kind of intense introspective nature. There is a time—call it the "moment of truth," if you like—when just as the bullfighter must show he is in command, so the director must indicate that as sympathetic as he is to the subject, and God knows I was that, he must express a kind of parental disapproval. He is challenged. He must respond, or all is lost. This was that moment in this film. To have waited in the wings for possible tantrums would be to lose control of the film. Its potential was so great, I decided to risk all.

I gave my instruction to Ken Gregg, my extraordinary cameraman, and he has heard something similar to it in each of a dozen of these works since. "Wrap it. We leave in the morning, first thing."

And so, early, at about seven the next morning, Bryan, on cautious toes, pinned a note to Tennessee's door: "Sorry you are not feeling well. Filming will stop for the moment. We will try again at a later date. With appreciation, Harry." There was no sign of movement in the Tennessee compound.

We set out on the long journey home. Somewhere along the highway to Miami, across those endless narrow bridges that link the Florida Keys, which seem like the afterthought of America, I paused to make a phone call to Billy Barnes in New York. Billy told me that Tennessee had already been on the phone to him asking what had happened, expressing his sorrow at our departure and his wish to see me again.

It had been a difficult decision. But after that time, there never was an angry or apprehensive moment with him. I think he knew that I had a certain strength; he had tested it, and now we really could be friends. That seemed to have become as important to me as the film had been in my mind. To have experienced the kindness of Tennessee was something no one could ever forget. His life force was so enormous that it filled any room he inhabited, and in the case of the film it transcended the medium.

Now it was up to me to find ways of enhancing the beginnings, to give the drama of his life its full possibility. There would never be anyone like him again.

Emotionally fragile as he was, Tennessee came north, this time to allow himself to be presented with an honorary degree, a Doctorate of Literature from the University of Hartford. We taped the proceedings. The introduction by the head of the department of communications and theater was suitably sober and laudatory. To quote some of it: "Mr. Williams, we take the occasion of the twenty-fifth anniversary of *A Streetcar Named Desire* to express our enormous appreciation of your achievements. Your work assures you of a permanent position among the great writers of American Literature. Your work, in your own phrase, 'arrests time.' It enables us to confront the enormous grotesqueries of the world with insight and compassion. Through your plays we discover our own loneliness and isolation and come to know the restorative power of our own imagination. You show us that life can be bestial and beauti-fragile, but art—your art—can redeem life by seeing it whole and deep and significant."

Tennessee decided to play it medium cool. He looked for laughs and got them. He played the comic. He said he had checked the program. "Now, let's see here," he said. "Oh, I'm almost the last thing on the program. Then there's going to be music provided by the Hartford College of Music. Now, I don't want to delay that music long. And I hope it's suitable, something like the 'St. Louis Blues,' or I'd be even happier to settle for 'Dixie.' "

The laughter was loud and regular. Tennessee was enjoying being the performer. He recalled, "I had trouble with projection when I was on the stage recently as an actor. Coincidentally, the part I was playing was called Doc. And he was a doctor who had lost his license. Yuh know, for practicing under the wrong conditions, which involved inebriation. I've come here sober. Well, now I'm a legitimate doctor, yuh see. I guess that's a wisecrack, and I don't know if it belongs in a convocation address. But since I don't have a convocation address, I guess that any little treasure of wit thrown in will be fully appreciated."

Since he did not, as he said, have a properly composed address, he read instead from his then-still-unpublished *Memoirs*. He chose as his reading of the day the description of how *Streetcar* came together as a work. He spoke of the time at Cape Cod when he came up with the closing line. He said, "We'd come to the Cape too early for ocean bathing. It was still icy-cold in the ocean. But I continued working on *Streetcar*. And it was in that cabin that I thought of the the exit line of Blanche, which later became quite historical. 'I've always depended upon the kindness of strangers.' Actually it was true. I always had, and often had been disappointed. In fact, I would guess that chance acquaintances or strangers have usually been kinder to me than people that know me well."

The transcript of the day has marked in "heavy laughter," which seemed to encourage him. He continued, "To know me is not to love me. At best, it is to tolerate me. And of drama critics I would say that the talent is now worn out, or I would not be writing my life story."

And so he went on, concluding with the story of how he met Brando, and how he fixed both his plumbing and electricity, and how he was the handsomest man he ever saw. He finished off by saying, "The New York opening was a smash. Well, I was called on the stage opening night for a bow, as I had been for *Menagerie*. . . . I was equally awkward about it. I believe that I bowed to the actors instead of the audience. . . . I think it's now time for that jazz."

Of course, the audience enjoyed him and his self-deprecating remarks. Sadly, I think. More powerfully than at any time in his existence, Tennessee needed a stronger adviser to insist that he not provide ammunition for his detractors. His record was and is still unequaled in theatrical history; only Shakespeare wrote more quality work.

In his closing remarks that morning, Mr. A. M. Woodruff said, "Mr. Williams, you have made a whole generation of Americans understand themselves a little better. They stand just a little straighter."

Tennessee, in that period of adjustment, just couldn't seem to hear this kind of adulation. If only he had.

I shuffled back and forth from New York to Toronto to Key West in the months that followed, attempting to dramatize excerpts from his work. With the exception of Brando, whom I never could locate, each actor was most pleased to participate, each working for far less than his or her normal rate. This despite Tennessee's observation that "I have always been awkward and diffident around actors so that it has made a barrier between us almost but insuperable." Perhaps there was a personal barrier. But I think each of his stars was so moved by the parts he created for them that a request to appear in a film with him and about him was like a command performance.

To Key West I brought Jessica Tandy to repeat her magnificent rendition of Blanche. She came with her inseparable husband, Hume Cronyn. So close have they grown as a theater couple that each seems to mouth the words of the other. They have a bond like the perfect lyric to a song, wonderful to watch and listen to.

I recall we went to dinner the night prior to the performance, and Hume told me the story, then not commonly known, that he had been perhaps the first backer of Tennessee's work. He had paid an option fee of fifty dollars a month for production rights to nine of his one-act plays. He said that the plays had haunted him because of their poetic nature. Hume was and is a man of incredibly fine taste. Both he and the gentleman producer Robert Whitehead are of distinguished heritage from London, Ontario.

On this occasion, Hume arrived with the portion of the play that I had selected for dramatization, fully prepared for Jessica. He had in fact worked with her for many hours. Of course, Jessica had been the original and perfect Blanche. Although Vivien Leigh had great power in the film, which had been denied Jessica, she still was perhaps too stagey. Jessica had found the poetic pulse exactly, the rhythm of the language playing to silent instruments. Hers is the performance by which every Blanche must be judged.

I had decided to stage the reading as a soliloquy in Tennessee's patio-garden. My theory, which I had developed in earlier films such as *Hall of Kings* in Westminster Abbey and *Upon This Rock* in St. Peter's in Rome, is that the setting, the real place—in this case the actual home of the playwright—adds that extra power to the performance. It becomes almost sacred.

Blanche, of course, is perhaps the most sacred of all of Tennessee's creations. The question now was, could Jessica, twenty years older than she had been at the time of the original Broadway debut, make the magic happen again? I had blended two of her best speeches together. I arranged for the garden to be lighted by colored lanterns, the stuff of memory. Her dress was a sort of nightgown of magenta, in muted tones.

Hume, to his credit, did not come to the actual film recording. He was like an expectant father, pacing the floor of the Pier House Hotel room as we worked through the night. There was only one problem to set straight. Since the speeches had been delivered to other real actors on stage, who was she, in fact, talking to?

I gave her only one piece of direction, which I thought might make the dramatization easier. I said, "Jessica, pretend that you are Blanche twenty years later, and perhaps you have been in the rest home or mental hospital to which she was sent, and someone stops you and asks, 'Blanche, what happened?' Tell him with all your heart everything that has been tightly held within yourself. Tell him with all your passion what happened."

It was incredibly effective. Years dropped from her as she paced the measured stone. She seemed almost airborne, gliding through the lines. And I recall when she said the words, when she embraced the characters, the very real person of Blanche, it was as if in fact she were on stage, in front of cameras, surrounded by great audiences, and the true power and poetry of Tennessee Williams filled that patio and Key West and the world. The real pain of Blanche, exposing her inner anguish, her confession of torment, was an outcry never to be forgotten, (And inevitably, when the finished film is shown, there is spontaneous applause for the greatness of performance and language.) You could well recognize why Brooks Atkinson, in his original review in *The New York Times*, said, "This must be one of the most perfect marriages of acting and playwriting. For the acting and playwriting are perfectly blended in a limpid performance, and it is impossible to tell where Miss Tandy begins to give form and warmth to the mood Mr. Williams has created. . . . Mr. Williams . . . has not forgotten that human beings are the basic subject of art. Out of poetic imagination and ordinary compassion he has spun a poignant and luminous story."

It may be worth recalling that in that same review Brando is only mentioned in passing as being of "high quality."

There was one line I had hoped to include in the soliloquy, but it just did not fit in, and that was Tennessee's expression about love, "And suddenly there is God." I felt that way about that performance that night of the colored lanterns. The creator of the words had brought us closest to our creator with that language and with that perfect performance of those ideas. God waited in the wings.

If Blanche is Tennessee's best-known female creation, really part of our language now, then there's no question that his most famous male character is Big Daddy of *Cat on a Hot Tin Roof*. Big Daddy is the swaggering biblical powerhouse who is part Tennessee's father and part patriarch. He has a monarch's lines.

I had wanted to dramatize some of his speeches.

(Ain't that forever Big Daddy?)

The play was not available, but Big Daddy was. Because of various legal complications it became impossible to stage or use any part of *Cat*. But one phone call to Burl Ives was enough to have him ready and able. He said flatly about Tennessee, "I will do anything for that man," and meant it.

It was decided that we would stage part of *The Last of My Solid Gold Watches*, and for the sake of convenience we would film it in Key West, despite the fact that the actual setting is the Delta.

Burl explained to me that it had been Tennessee's confidence that had made the role of Big Daddy possible for him. Until that time he was considered chiefly a singer of songs, a great one, but not an actor. Tennessee had seen in this gentle, awesome-looking man the personification of the character he was looking for: a booming drum of an actor.

He was a man of huge appetites in real life, an admirer of women and food and full living. During our short period together, I witnessed his constant battle with sugar-plum fairies. He had ice-cream eyes. He was also having some difficulty with memorization, which meant having to rethink our style of telling the story. But there was no doubt that this was Big Daddy and "Mistuh Charlie" combined.

After a humid day of filming, we sat in the hotel room in Key West and Burl sang for us songs of the South, authentic melodies that might suggest themes later on for the musical score of the film. It was extremely helpful, as we discovered. The small play set a mood for the passing of time and the slow decay of the South and a period of lost elegance and large dreams that was fading.

It was, I think, during this period of filming that I attended a dinner party in Key West with Tennessee and the younger playwright Lanford Wilson. Recalling the time of his youth when he had been a wanderer, Tennesse drafted some notes about his observations. These notes were in turn made into a television drama by Lanford Wilson called *The Migrants*. It was, I suppose, fair drama but seemed to have none of Tennessee's poetry and little of Wilson's trademark. The story still has never been told better than it was in Edward R. Murrow's famous "See It Now" documentary *Harvest of Shame*. What I remember most about the dinner was how patient and considerate Tennessee was with Wilson, giving advice and listening. He always seemed to have time for that.

Later Lanford Wilson would pay his dues to the master. He said, "I, like almost everyone of my generation, went into the theater because of my exposure to Tennessee. In high school, we did those ridiculous, old-fashioned comedies, and then I got to play Tom in *The Glass Menagerie*, and it was then I fell in love with the theater." I don't think Tennesse ever really accepted the impact he had on a generation of writers and actors.

His compassion crossed the footlights. He found it even for his parents who had done such a splendid job of orphaning him early on. About his mother, the dancing damselle Edwina, he was amazingly discreet most of the time. He said, "She had the gift of the gab. I must say she contributed a lot to my writing—her forms of expression, for example. And that underlying hysteria gave her great eloquence. I still find her totally mystifying and frightening. It's best we stay away from our mothers."

But even so, he expressed real concern about her right up until her very end, concern about her senility. He was concerned, but I think not forgiving, for what she had done both to his sister and to himself.

Tennessee spoke about the death of his father. The widow with whom he had been keeping company sat silently in the back row. The Delta drummer was dead, and Tennessee forgave him his long-distance sins.

How to give the simple truth of *The Glass Menagerie*, with its famous introduction of the relationship between truth and illusion, within the limited context of my film was my next problem, and it probably was the least successful part of it. I reasoned, perhaps falsely, that I could record a portion of it in a small way, playing it almost like an amateur production, because it had become the most-produced play of its kind in the world. No school, no town anywhere, had not had its own try at capturing the delicate destiny of the characters in *The Glass Menagerie*.

I wanted to capture what Tennessee described as "the open sky of my youth."

In his opening soliloquy, Tennesse described the Gentleman Caller as the most realistic character in the play, being the messenger from a world of reality that his family was somehow set apart from. But since he said he had a poet's weakness for symbols, he was using the character also as a symbol: he was the long-awaited but always hoped for something we all live for.

The Gentleman Caller is the dream, the winning lottery ticket, the gift from the long-lost uncle, the hero on the white horse, the dream girl come to recognize your inner beauty within the plain exterior. I reasoned I could mix him in with the "folks" from St. Louis by having someone from another country, and thus I cast Michael York, who was visiting New York at the time. His glistening blond surface, I thought, might make him suitably exotic, which may or may not have been the thing to do. The girl for Laura, the crippled sister, came from a production in Florida—her name was Carol Williard. Perhaps she had done it in too much of an extreme on stage, but God knows she was frail, frail as tissue paper. James Naughton, although too tall, was an amiable Tom. What mattered most was that we had Maureen Stapleton to play the mother, Amanda. I think it is impossible for Maureen to give a bad performance. She is simply one of the great natural actors of her generation. She seems to have been written in person by Tennessee. Maybe she was.

Our problem was the setting. Short of budget, I tried to set up the illusion of a St. Louis apartment in a small suite at the Algonquin Hotel. We had almost no control over light. But really to provide for Tennessee's request, to capture the whisper in the air, light is needed. From his stage directions was the instruction to make all look like a religious painting by El Greco.

Yes, we were a little short of El Greco. In fact, when Maureen arrived on the set—that is, at the hotel room—she made a fast judgment and I think quite wisely said, "Better send for a couple bottles of wine." With or without wine, she was wonderful. In the case of Michael York, an accomplished actor, I think his hair was too long and his accent too short. But he was trying hard, trouper that he is. But the entire exercise did allow us to provide material for the real star, Tennessee himself, which we would be able to intercut from his prerecorded performance of the opening and closing, recorded many weeks earlier in New Orleans. His spirit was there at the Algonquin that day.

A description of *The Glass Menagerie* that I quite like was written by *Time* magazine in its cover story on Tennessee of March 9, 1962, in the days when it looked as if his glowing flight would go on forever:

> Says Williams: "It takes five or six years to use something out of life. It's lurking in the unconscious—it finds its meaning there." Essentially, Williams has been chosen by his subjects.
>
> *His Life is a Play*. The play that best proves it is *The Glass Menagerie*. In it, Williams held a mirror up to memory and caught upon it the breath of three lives: his mother's, his sister's and his own. In a lower-middle-class apartment in a Midwest-

ern city, Amanda Wingfield ("an exact portrait of my mother," says Williams) tries to cope with a peevish present by chattering of a fancied past. The son Tom (Williams) suffocates in a shoe factory and goes to movies to daydream of escape. The daughter Laura (Williams' sister Rose) has a mind and a personality as fragile as the little glass animals that deck her room. But the mother dragoons Tom into bringing home a marriageable "gentlemen caller" for Laura. When the caller turns out to be engaged, and unintentionally breaks the pet unicorn in Laura's menagerie, the girl's future can be read in the fractured glass. At play's end, Tom lunges free of family, but for the playwright-to-be the future would always be trapped in the past.

Like any biographical sketch in the popular press, this was an oversimplification. But it caught certain truths.

The other giant of the American theater of our time, Arthur Miller, elegantly summed up the excitement caused by *The Glass Menagerie* in a tribute in later years. Tennessee paved the way for so many.

It is usually forgotten what a revolution his first great success meant to the New York theater. *The Glass Menagerie* in one stroke lifted lyricism to its highest level in our theater's history, but it broke new ground in another way. What was new in Tennessee Williams was his rhapsodic insistence that form serve his utterance rather than dominating and cramping it. In him the American theater found, perhaps for the first time, an eloquence and an amplitude of feeling. And driving on this newly discovered lyrical line was a kind of emotional heroism, he wanted not to approve or disapprove but to touch the germ of life and to celebrate it with verbal beauty.

Arthur Miller and Tennessee Williams admired each other, but their life-styles were so vastly different, they seldom spoke.

This question of form now haunted me for months to come. No matter how we battled our raw film material in the editing sessions with master film editor Arla Saare, the film would somehow go off in its own direction. There was no way of following the traditional lines of starting at the beginning and chronologically proceeding with the telling of the story as biography. *Memory* became the key word. Once we allowed the memory to drift back and forth in time as it does in life, the lyric visual quality became obvious. The film had to be more like a poem than a narrative. Although I would hesitate to use such a phrase, it was a fact. We were structuring a film poem. That was and is its power.

That also became clear at the music stage. We settled upon a music recording with a full and accomplished score by the sensitive composer Louis Applebaum. But it was too formal for the subject. During a lunch break we began reworking it, including some of the film music ideas suggested by Burl Ives earlier. "Where does he come from, where does he go?" sung by Brenda Gordon, became a haunting theme that seemed to wind around the images like draped Spanish moss. And Moe Kaufman, Canada's leading jazz musician, added his own freely expressed sound to the sounds of the streets of New Orleans, giving the film a beat and rhythm that are natural and spontaneous.

By some mystic miracle, the film was scheduled for its first television release in Canada on March 26, Tennessee's birthday. The bureaucrat in charge of placement and timing knew nothing about Tennessee's birth date. So see what you can make of that!

Meantime, however, before the curtain could rise on the year of work that I had put into the film *Tennessee Williams' South*, another event had to take place in the natural and predestined ways of the world. *Out Cry* was scheduled to open at the Lyceum Theatre in New York on March 1, 1973. How desperate Tennessee had been to see it open and open well! But the compromises that were made had long before doomed it. That drama itself was its own kind of Greek tragedy. He had hoped to have the remarkable French-Canadian actress Genevieve Bujold star in it. I had worked with her in my film on Shaw and found her constantly exciting and imaginative, with an enormous purring sexuality about her. Tennessee recalled meeting her in Billy Barnes' apartment and saying to her, "You're beautiful! And slightly mad!" But she could not or would not do it. There had been talk about the highly skilled British actor Paul Scofield taking the male lead. He would have had the experience to find the inner strength for the wildness of the part, but he also was not available. The set that was designed for Peter Glenville's limp production looked like a reject from an Oscar broadcast in the days of radio. The instructions for the setting were clear; Tennessee said that the stage had to be set to show not only a distressed mind near its breaking point, but also show the nightmarish world we inhabit. What's so complicated about that? Let us just look around at the haunted world we live in and we have it.

At any rate, at that time Tennessee and I seemed to be on opposite tracks of satisfaction, our pendulums swinging to extremes. For my own work of the moment, I was feeling a sense of great accomplishment. For him, during the opening night of *Out Cry*, hell seemed to be in the air.

In *Memoirs* he wrote his moan and plea: He felt his life depended on that production. He said it was the last objective of his life in the theater. He prayed for it.

He had resorted to his own religious beginnings, trying to find meaning where none seemed clear. Like Job, cursing the curses upon him. Like Jacob, wrestling with angels. He was like Ahab, caught by the great white Moby Dick, unable to let go.

Sitting in the audience, watching the dreadful staged drama unfold, I was too callow or shallow to realize the extent of the pain he was feeling. After all, I reasoned, he was considered the greatest playwright in the world, he had earned millions of dollars by his pen, an accomplishment unequaled by any other writer for the theater—how could bad reviews of one play damage that much? But I was wrong and now weep for my own limited understanding.

When the curtain descended, an exhausted Tennessee crumbled down the stairs, a look of anxious agony in his hurt eyes, and he headed for the exit, and he kept going on to the South, south to Key West and anywhere he could hide.

Near the end of *Memoirs*, he says he considered *Out Cry* a major work and its misfortune on Broadway had not altered that personal appraisal of it. He says it took him a year to recover from the production and perhaps he never did.

I think it was at the wake at Sardi's after the fall, as it were, that night, that for the first time someone addressed me as ''Mr. Williams,'' confusing me with the absent playwright.

''Interesting play,'' the stranger said.

I don't know what I answered.

Why he suffered so, why he had to keep proving he was capable of creation, no matter that he had created the greatest body of work of its kind, he defined himself after philosophizing about the agony of *Out Cry*.

For him it was simply the need to create that he believed brought him closer to God. Once again, I was surprised how close this was to Ecclesiastes 3:22. "Wherefore I perceive that there is nothing better, than that a man should rejoice in his own works; for that is his portion: for who shall bring him to see what shall be after him?" Who indeed?

God seemed a long way from Broadway that night.

Within ten days, *Out Cry* was not even memory for the Broadway public. It closed after twelve performances.

Meantime, on the evening of March 26 at 8:30, the film *Tennessee Williams' South* was telecast across Canada in prime time. I had gone to one of the city's leading hotels as the guest of honor to view the premiere with members of the Shell Oil Company, the sponsor. Everything was perfectly arranged: caviar and champagne and meat done to perfection. But someone had neglected to test the TV reception. As a result, the two dozen guests viewed a blurred image of the entire film. I tried constantly to adjust the set but am not mechanically inclined. But even with the soft focus, I became aware that each of the women, the wives of the oil executives and advertising specialists, had tears in their eyes.

"What an amazing, feeling man," one woman said. "Thank you."

When I returned home with Arlene, feeling somewhat disappointed at the improper viewing conditions, there was a long list of telephone calls waiting. Among these was one from the wife of the program director, a quiet, stately woman, Nan Benson; she said she had never made a call following a TV show. She said simply, "You have done a beautiful thing about a beautiful man."

Among women and men who were willing to reveal their own tenderness, there seemed to be a national outpouring for the gentle forces they saw revealed. No tricks or mendacity could hide the suffering this man had done for humanity. The Canadian critics were especially kind. In a stunning piece in Canada's largest circulation daily, *The Toronto Star*, the able and articulate Jack Miller wrote a warm tribute that was headed simply, "Tennessee Williams: A Brilliant Account." I quote it here not to be self-congratulatory but merely to indicate the impact the film had, in contrast to the suffering Tennessee was personally experiencing across the border that very night.

Jack Miller wrote:

Open letter to Harry Rasky: About your film, *Tennessee Williams' South*, on the CBC at 8:30 tonight: Now look, Harry—you know I'm busy. I've got all these TV shows to watch and the radio to listen to and all the interviews to do, and there's this mountain of mail from the networks, and the phone's going all the time. And you know I'm a slow writer, so it takes a few hours to get this column together every day. So if you had to do a show on the playwright, couldn't you have settled for doing just a good, respectable job? That way, I'd have been able to give it the standard 90-minute look and write a paragraph or two about it and then get on with my other work. Did you really have to make this the greatest documentary on a living person that I'd seen, anywhere in the TV world in 20 years of looking? Did you have to break the patterns? Did you have to make it so I'd sit there, stunned, at the end, enchanted by what you'd shown me of the man's work, but so disturbed because now I realized how much of his artistry I'd missed? Why did you have to talk Williams himself into reading his own poetry so beautifully? I never even knew before that he wrote poetry, so I didn't worry about it—but now I've got this insatiable itch to get the full book on the man and savor every word. Why did you have to squeeze that great musical score out of Lou Applebaum? Why did you have to get that all-star cast (especially Burl Ives) to do the excerpts from his plays? I'd have been satisfied before just to look at the movies. Now I have to read it all.

It's that itch again. You've infected me with an itch for Williams' brilliance. It's going to take time—all that reading. And busy people don't have time. Didn't anyone ever tell you that work this good should be saved for the theatre? You don't give this sort of thing away free on television. Harry, you complicate life for me.

I was most pleased to complicate Jack Miller's life.

Warmed by the glowing reviews, I packed a film print of the broadcast and headed west to meet with Tennessee at the Beverly Hills Hotel. We each had other things that were bringing us to Los Angeles. He had gone to see a new twenty-fifth-anniversary production of *Streetcar* with Faye Dunaway and Jon Voight. I was to have a meeting with two wonderful friends, the great actor Sam Jaffee and his wife Bettye, and the impressive voice and colleague Lorne Greene, about joining me in Israel for a production I had long planned called *Next Year in Jerusalem*.

We arranged to have a screening take place in the same Beverly Hills Hotel theater where Tennessee had seen *The Wit and World of G. Bernard Shaw* a year earlier. Billy Barnes suggested a drink beforehand at the Polo Lounge bar. I was still feeling high from the Canadian debut but admit to some nervousness at now sharing the film with the subject. He must, of course, be the final judge. It is indeed presumptuous for anyone to say to another human being, this is your life—this is the essence of you as seen and felt by me.

Gus, the great Greek bartender, was in command. And I recall distinctly that Tennessee was preoccupied. He was still talking about the review of *Out Cry* that had appeared in *Time* magazine a week earlier. I had skimmed through it on the American Airlines flight on the way west. I thought at the time that it was a minor blow to a career that could never be challenged. But now, in retrospect, I realize what a crucifixion it was. After all, this was the same magazine that had praised him with its highest accolades two decades earlier with a cover story that glowed like a national neon light, praising him as the "consummate master of theater . . . the greatest living playwright anywhere." Yesterday I went to the library to find the review that had caused Tennessee to say, "I must write the critic, T. E. Kalem, and tell him what I meant. I must make him understand." Billy and I argued against it. Now I know why Tennessee felt so savaged. The review had the headline "The Crack-Up." Judge this judgment:

The more perfect the artist, the more completely separate in him will be the man who suffers and the mind which creates.

T. S. Eliot

It is because Tennessee Williams once was just such an artist that the appearance of *Out Cry* is immensely saddening. Here, the man who suffers and the mind which creates are no more separate than a drunk and his crying jag. In the plays that earned Williams his reputation as America's finest dramatist, he showed that he could impose the order of art on his darkling terrors and forge passion and compassion out of pain. *Out Cry* is devoid of those gifts.

Insofar as this play has a psychological terrain, it is limbo. Symbolically, a spiral staircase on the stage ends in mid-air, leading nowhere. Two actors, a brother (Michael York) and a sister (Cara Duff-MacCormick) have been deserted by the rest of their company on a tour of some unnamed country. In panic they improvise "The Two Character Play," a misty memory of a long-past family in a southern U.S. city that culminated in the murder of their mother by their father and his suicide.

Most of this is rendered in maundering monologues and non-sequiturish asides. A Williams groping for words, parched for images, fumbling in dramatic craft—all this seems incredible, but alas, it is true.

Not then, not ever, did Tennessee "grope for words." It was what I called an "assault on a major."

With the critical world attacking him, it is not surprising that Tennessee chose to fortify himself with a couple of drinks and as many friends as he could gather around at the screening. I recall a subdued Michael York and his wife were in attendance. *Out Cry* was his first and last Broadway bow. Faye Dunaway arrived looking dark-haired and dark-eyed with her jazz musician friend of the day. Christopher Isherwood, the longtime friend and writer, showed up in quiet style. The Professor, Oliver Evans, now back at school after his journey to the Orient, seemed as excited as a schoolboy. I had an assorted group of relatives. Thom Benson, the CBC executive who had been my chief supporter, made a short introduction. But Tennessee was impatient and anxious: "Can we have the film speak for itself?" And so we began.

He sat, I think, with a kind of astonishment. He passed comment on the visual beauty. He loved the tender quality of the female Negro voice of Brenda Gordon that accompanied the shots of the

Mississippi. He praised the performance of Burl Ives, indicating to me that he did not mind my eliminating a minor character, so Burl was free to address the camera. He felt the sequence from *The Night of the Iguana* was an improvement on the film by John Huston because the sequence I chose had been done as a flashback. He liked the dark quality of John Colicos and the serene and solid beauty of Colleen Dewhurst.

When the second reel began, he grasped my hand as he listened to his own voice accompanied by music for the reading of the poem "Shadow Wood." He said, "Why, Harry, you've given me MGM treatment," and laughed. He expressed some concern about the modern painting background for William Hutt's rendition from *Small Craft Warnings* but thought Hutt's performance perfect. When Jessica made her film entrance, he called out, "She's better than she ever was." About the questionable *Glass Menagerie* sequence, he was polite but protested the setting: "It ain't St. Louis!"

The film concluded with a montage of photographs of Tennessee throughout his life and my narrative:

> The Bravos come in the form of honors, Pulitzer Prizes, and the friendship of the famous. But the ultimate applause must come from you, if you are to be a traveller in that distant, dark poetic place that is in all of us—Tennessee Williams' South—in feeling the emotion that is the last line of his very human outcry that magic is the habit of our existence.

The theme music then filled the room, the longing hum of the saxophone and the voice of the black singer asking again and again, "Where does he come from and where does he go?"

Then, there are sunset shots from the Pier House at Key West of shrimp boats going out to sea, the kind of boat that I assumed some day would take Tennessee's remains to rest.

The directions on my script read: "Closing credits appear over shots of a shrimp boat in the setting sun, heading out to sea, the restless, changing, comforting sea. A last voyage."

When it was all over there was a call of "Bravo." He turned to me. He hugged me and laughed that nervous laugh and said,

"Well, Harry. It's beautiful, especially given the subject. It's a relief. Why don't we go eat?"

And so the saki flowed. We adjourned to a nearby Japanese restaurant so the Professor could continue his Oriental period. Tennessee was glowing in a peaceful way. He sat next to me. "Well, Harry, you really didn't do it, after all."

He had been waiting, waiting since the filming began, to see if the trust he had put in me would be deceived. Even as we sat there, a new interview had appeared in *Playboy* that was the usual savage study of the fallen idol disappearing into depravity.

"You didn't get into the sex thing. I waited. You didn't do it."

I reminded him of what he himself had written in a *New York Times* piece just a couple of weeks earlier. He said, "I have never found the subject of homosexuality a satisfactory theme for a full-length play, despite the fact that it appears as frequently as it does in my short fiction. Yet never even in my short fiction does the sexual activity of a person provide the story with its true inner substance."

This had been my own reasoning, more or less. Whatever he was creatively had little to do with his sexual preferences or lack of them. He was after the sham and mendacity of our lives, the outer surfaces that mask our inner lies, and emotional turmoil. What he had to say about homosexuality, I still feel, was best expressed in dramatic form with splendid eloquence in the speech of Quentin in *Small Craft Warnings*, and no play has appeared on Broadway since that time that has risen to the heights of self-realization of that great aria.

How deeply he felt about my not taking advantage of his openness and confessional he expressed with simply stated facts in his *Memoirs*. After recounting his bizarre experience with a Fräulein from German television, who seemed out of Wagner, he briefly gave his version of our interlude. First, he explained his theory of why he was such choice game for TV interviews. He wrote with candor.

He said that the German woman, like so many commentators of the period of his public demise, would sit in comfort under an ample banana tree while he sat in the rain. He claimed the reason for the hostility of interviewers of this period was to trap the American playwright who had become so notorious. He said it obviously appealed to their sadistic nature, and that frankly he was getting bored with the sameness of the questions.

And then he commented about our mutual rapport. Again he said he was uncomfortable, but so was I. He said he was drenched with sweat, which was true, because our time together was hot. But he had noticed that I sweated along with him and did not take shelter under any spreading banana tree.

It has long been and still is my policy to make the subject as casually relaxed as possible, always finding the favorite spot or chair where the mind will let go. And at all times during the filming with Tennessee, I never tired him or let him feel that he was ever out on a line that I was enjoying except to achieve the mutual creative product. The film would link us for ever and ever.

Since reading the perceptive and warm comments, I have never passed a banana tree without a smile. In fact, maybe that's why I eat a banana for breakfast daily.

There was a bit of the banana-tree atmosphere loose the night of the long dinner. Oliver Evans glowed with excitement and seemed to want to lead a seminar. We became involved in a discussion of God. Oliver Evans was quite masterful in his analysis, despite his warning to me some months earlier not to be analytical of Tennessee because he suspects easy analysis. What he said that evening was a condemnation of what he had written to me after leaving Bangkok for Tokyo and Hong Kong. He was back teaching now, back to his last semester, and he wanted to be clear. He said:

> Tennessee, I imagine you were somewhat startled by what I wrote to Harry about certain resemblances between you and Hemingway, so I thought I'd amplify to you just exactly what I meant. The context concerned your respective religious attitudes. Neither Hemingway nor Whitman (whom I also included in my comparison) found it easy to believe in a personal God; they thought God was present in all of nature and more particularly in man himself. For divine love they substituted human love: "You're my God," Catherine Barkley tells Lt. Henry in *A Farewell to Arms*. And I'm sure you remember the scene in *The Sun Also Rises* where Jake and Brett enter a church and try to pray but cannot succeed; both of them envy the simple faith of the Spanish peasants to whom prayers come as easily as smiles

or tears. Modern man, "emancipated" man, Hemingway felt, could not accept literal dogma, and so for religious faith they substituted human love, which was as close to God, his characters seem to feel, as man could get. Rightly or wrongly, I feel that in a general way your characters are also like this. I remember your scoffing at Christopher Isherwood's praise of the line "I have always depended upon the kindness of strangers," and yet I too think it a great one; human love manifests itself through the kindness of strangers more eloquently than anywhere else. Of course, this trust is often misplaced—as it is in the case of Blanche, for the context there is ironical: the doctor's action in leading her offstage is professional and impersonal rather than *kind*. But how much better a world it would be if we *could* depend upon the kindness of strangers! The line expresses a great ideal, and that is why it is great.

"Oliver," said Tennessee, "you do get carried away. I think the Orient has gone to your head. I think the rice has been spiked. But this is a celebration."

"But, Tennessee, that is the point. All your best work celebrates life!" Oliver was emphatic.

It was a happy birthday party.

And Tennessee was ecstatic. I think I only once more saw him so relaxed and free of his inner demons. That was the night of the extraordinarily successful opening of *Tiger Tail* in Atlanta, about which I will write just a little later.

Of course, I was pleased, pleased and delighted. Surely, I thought, it will not be difficult to find a larger audience for the film, especially in the United States. Little did I suspect that soon I would feel like a tied-up iguana.

At first I thought, everything is going our way. As it happened at the time, there was a strange ruling at NBC, that provided that no program could be screened in advance of its air date by the newspaper critics. It was argued that an unsympathetic critic could diminish the size of the audience. By coincidence, an earlier epic film I had written and directed called *Upon This Rock* was having its premiere the following week on NBC. I was not totally pleased by the TV version, as it had been drastically cut from ninety minutes to fifty-five minutes. It was a little like providing half a dome. NBC was anxious to have some advance attention, and the local publicity person had arranged for the dean of the country's TV critics, Cecil Smith, to view *Tennessee Williams' South* as an alternative.

Cecil Smith's review was absolutely glowing. The headline was "Raskymentaries: TV for Posterity."

In part, he wrote:

> Harry Rasky's new documentary, "Tennessee Williams' South" was shown over the Canadian Broadcasting Corp. TV network on the playwright's 62nd birthday, March 26, to ringing acclaim. After which Rasky flew here from Toronto with the film under his arm to show it "to the toughest critic of them all: Tennessee."
>
> Williams was here for the new production of *A Streetcar Named Desire* with Faye Dunaway and Jon Voight at the Ahmanson—he has since fled to the Orient. Rasky was apprehensive about him seeing it. He needn't have been. Tennessee loved it: 'Let this be my epitaph!'
>
> With reason, I might add. Not only is the film a definitive statement on the life, the work, the attitudes and beliefs of Williams but in a documentary technique that has come to be known as "Raskymentary," the film segues from the man into scenes from his plays, each complementing the other.
>
> The scenes are performed by such illustrious actors as Burl Ives, Jessica Tandy, Maureen Stapleton, John Colicos, William Hutt and Colleen Dewhurst. Thus, an extraordinary factual document is an extraordinary entertainment. The question is when and if a film on American's greatest living playwright will be shown in America. Rasky shrugs. "In time," he says.
>
> He has astonishing patience for a tiller of TV's arid soil. TV is instant art. Off the story boards and onto the screens and forgotten. But not as Rasky practices it. He spends a year or more handcrafting each of his films. He feels he is creating not a momentary distraction but a permanent contribution to the culture of these times. Time, he says, is on his side.

I still accept the truth that time is on the side of my films. But I am older and more tired. The truth has its own special rhythm. It can't be hurried.

I made the rounds carrying the film under my arm to the three commercial networks. The various vice presidents smiled tolerantly. The idea of devoting ninety minutes to culture, even if it involved the country's number-one playwright personality, was rather ridiculous to them. (I think *they* were rather ridiculous!)

I next held a special screening in New York for the representative of one of the chief corporate underwriters for Public Broadcasting. Tennessee himself came to sit in a darkened screening room to lend his support. The smiles were even more secret. I later learned that the same executives who had deemed George Bernard Shaw too controversial because of his early pacifism (to World War I, for God's sake!), and thus against the Vietnam war, now were judging Tennessee not sponsorable because of his homosexuality. We were offered flabby explanations—mendacity incorporated.

"They're waiting for the corpse," said Tennessee. "I'm inconveniently alive."

So alive that he was of course on to other works. As a gift to me he had written *Stopped Rocking*, his first work directly for television. It was meant to be for me to direct and for the talented Maureen Stapleton to star in. It too began to make the rounds. Word kept coming back that no one was interested in Tennessee's unestablished new work, and who would want to see a film that takes place in a mental hospital?

If Tennessee was going mad, it seemed to me that he had good reason.

Perhaps they didn't know what his plays were about anymore.

As Oliver Evans wrote me in one of his long-distance letters: "We realize that in Williams' best plays, he constantly celebrates the vital principle, which usually triumphs. And it's precisely the conflict of the vital with the decadent, the positive with the negative, the constructive with the destructive, that gives his work its cosmic significance."

Cosmic and commercial apparently were two different matters. There seemed to be a kind of commercial blackmail against him.

In hope of causing some forward movement, he wrote a brief foreword for *Stopped Rocking*. He pointed out quite correctly that a piece of writing for the screen or TV is not finished until it also becomes the work of the director and the star. He was kind enough to refer to both Maureen Stapleton and myself as "masters in their

101

fields." He was sure there was a waiting audience for the work. He explained his feeling that it was a work of "humanity," in the same spirit as *The Glass Menagerie*, which was soon to reappear on TV with Katharine Hepburn and Michael Moriarty. He reminded the reader of the great success of *Menagerie*. He said he felt audiences needed these feelings again.

Need?

It would be two years before there was even a rumor of interest in either film. We gained an ally for *Stopped Rocking* at Universal Pictures, the great film factory in the foggy hills of California. Jules Irving, a tasteful and polite producer who had earned some fame when he jointly operated the theater at Lincoln Center, had moved out to California at the request of his brother, an executive at Universal. He was instructed to bring a little culture to the coast. But, I would now guess, not too much. To his credit, he was able to convince the men in gray who frequented the stubby skyscraper at Universal City to take an option on the property. An "option," I had learned during a brief fling a few years earlier in Hollywood, is like foreplay in sex, in which few orgasms ever take place. Much serious conversational petting leads to little action.

However, we went through the ritual of script meetings, casting meetings, and production meetings. It is a deathly depressing dance.

Tennessee, I think, knew from the start that it was a doomed exercise. Perhaps that is why he could bring along a quantity of marvelous, outrageous behavior. It was decided that having such a distinguished writer on the "property" meant that all the dark-suited producers, writers-who-long-ago-had-forsaken-their-dreams, would attend a command performance luncheon at which Tennessee and I were to be the guests of honor. The graying men whose ideals had hardened gathered in a plain white plastic dining room along a long table. In these sterile surroundings no one knew how to begin. Each knew his territory. The easy dollar had squashed the life out of the sanitized writers in the room.

Tennessee told the story that he later recounted in a different form in *Memoirs*. He said, "Yuh know, the last time I remember such an auspicious lunch out here, I was traveling with my close friend. The host was Mr. Jack Warner. Everyone in the room was introduced. Finally Mr. Warner stared at my dear friend and traveling companion and asked, 'What do you do, young man?'

"My friend obviously thought it was none of his business because he responded in a loud and certain voice, 'Why, I'm here because I sleep with Mr. Williams.'

"I think, you might say, that sort of broke the ice. . . . Kind of yuh all to come out to meet Harry and I."

I can't remember if there was any collective reaction. I think the group had production schedules on its mind. The era when a major writer could come to Hollywood and make an impact, as in the days of Faulkner and Fitzgerald, had passed. Nothing could shake the foundation of the glass god of Universal at its remote Burbank headquarters. Tours had taken over from taste long ago. *Jaws* and trick photography had taken over from story and content. Movies now were for thirteen-year-olds. *Pow!*

Our stay was pleasant. One night Tennessee went out with Isherwood and the boys. Out of deference to my own heterosexuality, he considerately said, "Harry, I want to spare you. You might want to pass over the evening's festivities."

Another evening we went to see a local production of *One Flew Over the Cuckoo's Nest*. The production was satisfactory but Tennessee caustically remarked, "I think this play has as much to do with madness and an asylum as does *South Pacific*."

He tried some rewrites to please the Universal powers. Jules Irving had a hopeful meeting with an actor I've always admired, Burt Lancaster, who eventually turned the project down. I still feel this was an error on his part because, as he told Jules, "This is a tough script."

Back in New York, some weeks later, there was a near scene with Tennessee. He had been calling me all over town. I got his message, strangely enough, while I was at Radio City Music Hall with my children. He insisted I join him immediately at the Elysée, which I did, after the stage show. I used to love to see the orchestra being lifted majestically from the pit to the stage.

In the Victorian Suite, he confronted me with an altered script, one that Jules in all innocence had compiled from various rewrites. He looked at me as directly as he could and asked, "Harry, I want you to tell me—did you have anything to do with this?"

I looked back at him just as positively. "Look me in the eyes, Tennessee. You will find no mendacity there. I personally have not altered one word of your script. Not one word. I have not come all this distance with you to ever lie." And I never did.

Tennessee shrugged, exorcising Jules Irving and his executive brother. "The only brother act I ever cared for was the Marx Brothers."

We tried a reading with Maureen one evening at the Hotel Pierre. The script sounded exciting. Coming down in the elevator, Maureen said, "Come on, let's do it. Let's forget money and just do it."

I agreed. But no action was ever taken. More rewrites were ordered. Eventually Jules vanished more and more, and finally one day we were told he had died silently while playing tennis. And so a tiny try at culture left Universal City, and now only Porsches grow in its great tarred parking lot. Since that time, murder, homosexuality, cancer, and mental breakdowns have become the weekly menu of the ''Movie of the Week,'' sometimes now referred to as ''Disease of the Week.''

As time passed, I would journey to Jerusalem to film there. I would make a one-man show with Christopher Plummer in *Travels Through Life with Stephen Leacock*, the Canadian humorist, who, quite correctly, reminded us all that "Half a brick, like half a truth is much more powerful. It's easier to throw and carries further."

I felt that, if I had caught hold of some truth, I wanted to carry it as far as I could. In desperation, I had been scrutinizing the columns of *The New York Times*, searching for some kind of ally. I felt that the reviews of the chief cultural correspondent of the day, John Leonard, had a certain integrity and bounce about them. I called him with no ceremony. Just phoned. I said, "Please come and see a film I have made." To his credit, he came up the shoddy elevator of a decaying building of screening rooms on Broadway. There, between private screenings of porno films, I managed to squeeze in showings of both the Shaw and Williams films.

John Leonard became a supporter. In a Sunday *Times* review on June 13, 1976, he asked the various networks in print why my films had not been shown. In his closing line he said, "Perhaps they're ashamed that somebody in Toronto is doing better work than everybody in Los Angeles and New York. Color me perplex."

Perplexed indeed.

Mr. Shaw would have to wait a full decade before he found a place on U.S. television, and on a limited number of stations at that. But finally a request did come from the Eastern Education Network of PBS, which had suddenly discovered Tennessee. For a minimum amount of money, they would take the program. But it took all that effort and time.

Tennessee Williams' South was finally scheduled to be telecast in a limited U.S. run on the night of December 8. I went to New York that week to celebrate with Tennessee. He had been much in the spotlight. A couple of days earlier, one of the U.S. networks had carried a made-for-TV version of *Cat on a Hot Tin Roof*. Tennessee and I watched part of it together. There was great disappointment in the performance of Laurence Olivier; the greatest actor of the century simply seemed out of sync. He was like Nixon and so were his gestures. Olivier was about as southern as chicken chow mein. He was almost like a caricature of himself. It was as if he had swallowed a volume of *King Lear* and was trying to regurgitate it with an American southern accent. When he talked of being the owner of "twenty-eight thousand acres of the richest land this side of the valley Nile," you knew they must have been on the Thames, not on the Mississippi River. The *Daily News* said the film was like a "high-class greeting card."

The following night, Tennessee and I dined together before attending a sort of wake for an ill-fated production of *The Eccentricities of a Nightingale*, a variation of *Summer and Smoke* that had received a fine production earlier on PBS. Onstage at a seminar after the performance, he was very amusing but was disturbed by recent reviews. He asked me to take a bow from the audience and recommended that the audience watch my film the next night, saying that there was no advertising so he had to do his own. He asked me to quote something I had said at dinner from GBS's dustman character, Doolittle: "I ask you what am I? I'm one of the undeserving poor: that's what I am. Think of what that means to a man. It means he's up against *middle-class morality* all the time." Tennessee used that as his theme—his battle with the critics and their "middle-class morality."

He seemed relieved to have had the opportunity to express himself. A recent biographer claimed he went on for two hours and perhaps was drunk. I was with him before, during, and after, and this is nonsense. Since the symposium was at the Morosco Theater, we adjourned to Sardi's across the road. The next day's early edition of *The New York Times* was out. Under the heading "Depending on the Kindness of Public TV," John O'Connor began his flattering review:

> After being mistreated Monday evening on NBC's badly mangled and miserably cast production of "Cat on a Hot Tin Roof," Tennessee Williams is richly compensated tonight at 10 with a documentary on public television. Of course, the 90 minute portrait of the playwright and his work is more than three years old, but it was produced for the Canadian Broadcasting Corporation, which seems to be unusually sensitive and serious about writers. "Tennessee Williams' South" was produced, directed and written by Harry Rasky, whose credits also include a widely praised documentary on George Bernard Shaw. The Rasky technique is to combine direct biography with extended excerpts from the subject's writings. In this case, the playwright is the star, and Mr. Rasky has treated him well.

I read the review aloud, feeling much relieved. Tennessee listened carefully and said, "Well, it's all right. But the film is better than that. It should have been a better review, much better."

I was amused when I saw a review next day from *The Washington Post* that said, "Producer-Director Harry Rasky obviously had a high budget." Keep in mind my having had to shoot almost an entire act of *Glass Menagerie* in a boxlike Algonquin Hotel room.

Both the *Post* and *The Hollywood Reporter* made note of the irony that "this tribute to a great American artist was produced by the Canadian Broadcasting Corporation." *The Hollywood Reporter* called it an "almost transcendental experience," which is a phrase I like; it means that you are meant to feel you are there yourself without the intrusion of cameras or interviewer. It said, "This was an inspiring interview-exploration of the life and work of a man whom many would rank as our greatest living playwright."

But of all the reviews, the one I admired most was written by

Dan Sullivan, the *Los Angeles Times* theater critic. He caught what I was after exactly:

> Major writers don't just write deep, they write often, and in time they build up a world with its own peculiar light and breed of people. We start talking about Hemingway characters or Fitzgerald characters or Tennessee Williams characters. We start meeting them.
>
> Tennessee Williams' world combines the Deep South of his youth with the changeable weather in his own head. We get the feel of both in "Tennessee Williams' South," in a most satisfying TV documentary.
>
> "Documentary" suggests prose. Harry Rasky's film for the Canadian Broadcasting Corp. comes closer to poetry—strongly imaged, rhythmed, alive.

I became very grateful for the loneliness of the long-distance critic. In all, this film would be reviewed four different times by the *Los Angeles Times*, and each time the review seemed warmer. A year later, when I made a personal appearance with the film while on a promotion trip for my next major work, *Homage to Chagall—The Colours of Love*, the same Dan Sullivan said about it and the Williams film, "Each is worth a carton of biographies," and they lined up round the block.

But that night in New York we planned a small celebration. Despite his having viewed the film twice before, Tennessee arranged for a TV screening at the Victorian Suite. He had sister Rose specially brought into town. He placed her, rather lovingly, directly in front of the set. But no matter where he had her sit, her eyes never seemed to leave him in the room. She puffed away constantly, watching the TV world and her brother through clouds of smoke, a smoke of ages. What she saw and what she heard and what she felt I cannot tell you.

There was an amusing and troubling moment halfway through the film. The program abruptly came to a halt; the screen was filled with hawkers and promoters for PBS. We were being used for "pledge week." So not only had the stations paid a minimum, but they were using Tennessee's name for its selling power. There followed a parade of the famous opera singers and actors. I think Leonard Bernstein was especially elegant in seeking that viewers send along extra cash to help keep New York's Channel 13 in business. As time passed and a couple of glasses of wine were filled, the phone number kept flashing on the screen. Tennessee turned to me in cool anger and said, "Why, Harry, I think it's time for an obscene phone call!"

I dialed the number that was pulsating on the screen, and I told the gentleman who answered that I had made the film and was sitting with Tennessee and that he was growing impatient. Could they please hustle their commercials along? The man with whom I was speaking said, "I don't know who you are. But I don't believe you're with Tennessee Williams."

I relayed this information to Tennessee. Tennessee was furious. He insisted on having the phone. "Now, listen he'h. You have not paid me to be on your station. You are intruding on my friend Harry Rasky's beautiful film. Now yuh get all those people off there, so we can get on with the work in question. What's more, I don't think yuh have given Harry enough credit. He's worked hard on this film. Now, move those people off right away, yuh he'h!"

The man at the other end seemed stunned. He explained to Tennessee that he happened to be a vice president of WNET and had answered the phone by accident. He then made the mistake of asking Tennessee if he would come down and help get pledges for money.

Tennessee said, "I think that is hardly necessary, given your negligent payments to me. Get on with Harry's film. I have my sister Rose waiting."

No sooner had he hung up than the cast of assorted characters pleading for the impoverished station vanished. The film rolled on, and Rose continued to stare and stare at the Tennessee in the room and listen to the Tennessee on television.

When the film concluded, the announcer made a point of mentioning my name at least three times. Rose in the room said only, "Yes. Yes. Yes. Tom." She stared at me, with those eyes that seemed to lock onto your heart. I think that day in a way I had become his brother.

Tennessee would never test me again.

Our meetings, lunches and dinners, and occasional nights out were always for the simple pleasure of two friends getting together.

I felt our bond was unbreakable now. I think we supplied a kind of warmth to each other, a mutual caring. Yes, there was that expressed pain, physical and mental, that he suffered almost constantly. But it would be to miss the man not to know how rich was his sense of fun and feeling in his bittersweet existence.

I recall an evening we went to see *The Good Doctor* at the invitation of its star, Christopher Plummer, with whom I had worked several times. I had alerted Chris that we would come backstage after the performance for a drink in his dressing room.

I always enjoy Chris on stage, acting in the grand style, one of the best of our century. But *The Good Doctor* was something else, a reworking of some Chekhov pieces by Neil Simon, Moscow with a Brooklyn sense of humor. Tennessee's respect for Chekhov was such that he found the evening profoundly unfunny. He insisted that we leave at intermission. He agreed to dine early, during the second act, and drop in on Plummer afterward without revealing our exit before the final curtain. The dinner was the only time I ever actually saw him weep. Perhaps it had to do with a distorted sense of values as played out onstage. He said he had had a rebuff from some young man who had visited him that afternoon in his hotel room. He said, "I only wanted to express my love of beauty. Why couldn't he understand? Why can't they understand? I suppose, really, only women can give us the tenderness we require."

After dinner we went backstage, and he was back in fighting form. We entered the dressing room and were greeted by Chris and his devoted wife, Elaine. No mendacity tonight. Tennessee said, "I don't think Mr. Simon should tamper with brilliance, and that's why I left after the first act." I think Chris put it down to Tennessee being high. He wasn't. He just couldn't tolerate hypocrisy, the little lies that hold most of us together.

His focus on the larger areas of human feeling never allowed him to get involved in the dreary daily routines of existence. This question of getting lost anywhere. He seldom traveled alone. I recall that he wanted to see a French production of *Out Cry* that was being staged in Montreal and asked me to go along. He always assumed, like many American southerners, that Canada was somehow all the same city. Toronto and Montreal and Vancouver must be the same place. I couldn't make the trip but made the mistake of recommending he stay at the Bonaventure Hotel. I had admired the rooftop pool, which was heated in such a way that you could swim under the stars even during a snowfall. I thought it might appeal to his romantic spirit. But what I did not reckon with was his awkward sense of direction. The hotel is only the top few floors of a skyscraper, set on top of a huge underground shopping plaza, so Montrealers never have to go out and face the elements. Tennessee apparently took the elevator to what he thought was the lobby to buy some toothpaste and got lost for hours, thus almost missing the curtain. Someone had to rescue him. He summed up his experience at the rooftop pool: "I hated it." I've never been able to stay there since.

He kindly attended major creative functions in my own life. One evening, the Directors Guild of America was honoring me with the showing of my film *Next Year in Jerusalem* at its Fifty-seventh Street theater. We dined together with Arlene and two close friends of mine, two nonfiction writers, the beautiful and talented Carol Klein and her intelligent husband Ted, at Jimmy's, then owned by former deputy-mayor Dick Aurelio. After a fine and friendly meal, we decided to make the short walk to the movie house. When I looked behind, the entire group had gone astray. They had followed Tennessee, who obviously had no sense of where he was. He just always assumed someone would be there to lead or find the way. Perhaps it was left over from his childhood, when Ozzie, the colored maid, guided him and his sister. Or maybe he just felt reality was a place to be avoided. But I somehow never felt it was odd. About my film that night, he was quite correct. He said, "It's fine. But flawed." I had tried too hard.

On another occasion, he was proud of the fact that he had actually made it across town. I was having the first important preview of *Homage to Chagall—The Colours of Love* at a screening room at the Canadian Consulate in the Exxon building. I had gone by the Elysée Hotel to pick him up, but he had been delayed and was nowhere to be found. Just before curtain time, Tennessee emerged at the elevator, breathless and alone. "Made it. I made it." He seemed as proud as if he had had a new Broadway success. He joined in a conversation with Pierre Matisse, who was Chagall's New York representative. "A familiar name, Matisse. I paint sometimes. Do you?" Tennessee asked, good-naturedly.

Mr. Matisse smiled at his forthright quality. He said, "I am the junior. I paint sometimes when no one is looking."

They laughed together. Both men were especially kind to me that day. Matisse said, "I only wish you had been making films when my father was alive. What a wonderful record we would have."

Tennessee especially praised my script but said he would prefer the film to be called simply *The Colours of Love*.

I in turn tried to attend as many functions as possible in which he was involved. There was a brief ill-fated production of *The Gnädiges Fräulein*, now called *The Latter Days of a Celebrated Soubrette*. It was being staged in a dark, damp church hall. He actually insisted that I give some direction to the director. But it would do no good. The play lasted for one performance.

Oliver Evans had a theory as to why certain works by Tennessee were damned by the critics. He said that critics were against a play like *Camino Real* because "it was frankly allegorical and it's a play in which the characters are not interesting so much in themselves but because they stand for certain definite attitudes towards life."

Oliver wrote to me:

> Now I confess to a private liking for abstraction in the theater; it leads naturally to allegory, but allegory, being by nature didactic, has nearly always enjoyed a rather limited success. (I think this explains the commercial failure of *Camino*, which Tennessee has often called his finest play), It also, I am convinced, explains the coolness with which his latest plays have been received, for while Broadway will welcome allegory in a Continental playwright like Ionescu or Beckett (I think it's safe to think of Beckett as a French playwright) and even something as cryptic as *Tiny Alice*, by our own Albee, who has often acknowledged his debt to Tennessee, they have Tennessee "typed" for a certain kind of realism, and complain if they don't get it. Almost all the plays in *Dragon Country* exhibit this type of abstraction: the characters are grotesque because they are not intended to represent ordinary flesh-and-blood people, the kind who, like the Wingfields, live next door, but have been deliberately abstracted to serve as symbols of loneliness and despair. So many critics seem to have missed this point.

Actually the most perceptive critics were quick to grasp

the allegorical import of those plays which, like *Streetcar*, displayed an impressive surface realism: in that play one is conscious of the clash of vast, elemental forces much larger than the characters who personify them, and more universal; the abstractness, working subterraneously, accounts for much of the play's peculiar power. But abstract drama is intellectual drama, and intellectual drama, with a very few recent exceptions, has perhaps never been less popular than it is today.

Of course, virtually no recent work by Tennessee received kind comments. A great deal of the problem was in the productions themselves. The directors lacked strength. There was a great softness in purpose in the guiding hand. Kazan was never more missed. The sheer masculine drive of Elia Kazan had been enough to keep the definitions clear. There was no rambling off the edge of the stage.

On another occasion Tennessee asked me to sit in on a rehearsal of *Vieux Carré*. It was clearly doomed. If I may just put it crudely, "There were no balls in the direction."

Perhaps the only critic to stick with Tennessee to the bitter end was the immensely articulate Walter Kerr, who always judged Tennessee in relation to the huge body of his achievement. So he was able to write, even after the faltering reworking of New Orleans memories that became *Vieux Carré*:

> Tennessee Williams' voice is the most distinctively poetic, the most idiosyncratically moving, and at the same time most firmly dramatic to have come the American theatre's way—ever. No point in calling the man our best living playwright. He is our best playwright, and let the qualifications go hang.

He then went about weeping for the production at hand. The acting was strong but "The Angel in the Alcove," the story on which it was based, was never present. And a work that requires the lightness of the silvery dust of dream angels lies flat if it never gets airborne.

The next opening seemed even worse. When Tennessee spotted me at the box office before curtain time of *A Lovely Sunday for Crève Coeur*, he rushed over and hugged me. "Thank heaven I have a friend here, Harry."

When the curtain came down and the backers mounted to the upstairs at Sardi's, Tennessee was nowhere to be found. There was a really awkward moment. At the table at which I was sitting the gathered crestfallen Broadway angels began addressing me as "Mr. Williams" and telling me how much they had admired "my work." As much as I tried to stretch out my drawl, I felt too uncomfortable to yield any information or deny them their small hope that despite considerable financial loss they at least got to sit with the famous playwright for a while on opening night. Billy Barnes told me Tennessee was sitting down the road at a Broadway restaurant and asked if I could go and find him. I did. I urged him to drop in on the party. He did that. He came back for a trying wake.

I've often wondered what role I played in his life. I respected him totally. But it may also have been related to a need he talked about frequently to have someone to laugh with. We certainly did that. Even now.

I had always teased Tennessee about coming to visit me in Toronto, fully aware that he would never find his way. I recall asking him if he would attend my daughter Holly's Bat Mitzvah, knowing that this would be as likely as the Pope dropping by. So one day I was absolutely astonished to get a phone call at home: it was Tennessee and he was in Stratford, Ontario, attending a performance of Shakespeare. "I think we might all come on over for dinner tomorrow, if that's convenient with you and Arlene," he said. He had actually crossed the border.

We toured around the city. Tennessee pretended to marvel at the beauty of the clean city that is Toronto. I showed him the new City Hall, which is always shown to visitors, who are expected to remark at how stunningly modern it is. But Tennessee focused on the old City Hall and thought it quite beautiful. "I really like the old thing."

Toronto, they say, is a city that has a bank branch on every corner. "How clever," said Tennessee, trying to find a kind comment for the highly derivative city, "how clever to have a bank named after a fish!" He was referring to the Bank of Nova Scotia. Definitely not a place to buy your smoked salmon.

After dinner at a trendy dark restaurant, called The Three Small Rooms because the rooms were small (we tend to be literal up here—

the hospital for sick children is called The Sick Children's Hospital), we drove down to the Royal Alexandra Theatre, a building beautifully preserved by the local impresario "Honest Ed" Mirvish.

Sir John Gielgud and Sir Ralph Richardson were starring in a Pinter work. It was decided that we would all drop by and say hello after the performance. Sir John had directed the London production of *The Glass Menagerie*, and Ralph was Ralph. He had also starred in my film *Upon This Rock*, and he was one of the world's authentic eccentrics, a magnificent actor; he was also "the motorcycle lord."

We arrived just a little before the final curtain. I told the usher in charge that I had the world's greatest playwright with me and would he mind if we went in and caught the last few minutes of the show standing at the back? I wanted Tennessee to see the elegant decor. The young usher refused.

Then I saw Tennessee in an unfamiliar role. He stared at the young man with some scorn. But it was the kind of anger that he hoped would bring wisdom. He said to him, "When I was struggling to find my way in the theater, I too worked as an usher. The difference between you and me, young man, is that you will continue to be an usher."

Backstage, we were accorded a royal greeting from the two lords of the stage. Tennessee claimed that he was enjoying his Toronto visit and planned on spending several days. Unfortunately, I had to leave town, ironically heading south to Mississippi to hold some conversations with PBS officials about a possible film on Faulkner. "Faulkner," Tennessee told me, "had the saddest eyes of any man I have ever known."

About other contemporaries, by the way: He said that his meeting with Hemingway had been surprisingly cordial and that he found "Hemingway had a real gentleness about him." He never knew O'Neill. "I was not yet in the arena. I think he did well within his limited means." I think he meant vocabulary, but I would not be certain. He did say that he admired Pinter a great deal. "He knows how to write the pauses."

I delivered Tennessee back to the city's best hotel, the Four Seasons, and we said we would probably not see each other for a while.

Next morning at the airport, while checking in for a flight to

Oxford, Mississippi, I saw a tiny figure coming close in the almost deserted terminal. It was Tennessee.

"What happened?" I asked in some surprise.

"Well, Harry, first in Stratford I checked into a motel and no one would carry my bag. With my palpitations I don't think it wise to carry my own bag. Then there was that usher who wouldn't let me into the theater last night. Then this morning I woke up to do my usual writing before breakfast and I called down for a brandy. I sometimes like a glass of brandy beside me when I am working. I was advised that because it was Sunday there was something called 'the Lord's Day Alliance.' No liquor could be served. So I decided that this was not the place for a southern boy. We're skipping across the border. Good luck with Faulkner. At least dead writers don't talk back." He let out a sort of yelp of laughter and we parted.

There is a great snobbery among academics. Once they have latched onto "their author," all others somehow have to be diminished. In Mississippi, I found genuine hostility because I had formed a link with Tennessee, whom the Faulkner specialists regarded as a diminished talent. As for me, I know I should appreciate Faulkner more, but I always feel that I'm being sucked into a swamp when I encounter his prose. Needless to say, the Faulkner expedition went nowhere. And Tennessee was, as always, in transit.

He was restless, moving cities, friends, scripts, ill at ease with the world and frequently with himself. He was always trying to escape from sorrow, a sorrow that would not let him rest.

I had become deeply involved in the theatrical release of my film *Homage to Chagall*. It was extremely successful, and I thoroughly enjoyed having a banner flying over Fifty-seventh Street in New York, at the Little Carnegie Theater, announcing the victory. Perhaps it was a daily reminder to people in New York who knew me that I was just across the border, living still with the Lord's Day Alliance, along with the cold front from Canada.

But one day in the late months of 1977, the phone in my CBC office rang. It was Tennessee. He began, "Harry, I would like you to do something for me."

It was not a request I could refuse.

"Harry, there's this play. It's sort of based on the filmscript of *Baby Doll*. We plan on having a world premiere in Atlanta at the

Alliance Theatre down there, yuh know. If you can take time off from the studio up there, I would be pleased to have you direct it."

I said, "Of course, Tennessee, I'm flattered at the request. I will have to rearrange my life. I had planned on taking my family, Arlene and the kids, to Florida for a holiday around Christmastime."

"Bring them along, Harry. Or they can have my house in Key West. I need someone around I know and can trust."

For Tennessee to personally have made this call, I realized, took enormous need. First of all, the very fact that he could get through the complex long-distance and internal switchboards of the Canadian Broadcasting Corporation took perseverance unlike most of the daily occurrences in his life. Dialing a phone, for him, was like taking a transcontinental journey is for some others. He knew my stage experience was limited. He must have been up against some terrible problems.

As a formality, Billy Barnes sent me the script of *Tiger Tail*, which was the name of the *Baby Doll* rewrite, to study. It did mean some family juggling. I canceled the Miami holiday. Arlene was totally helpful. She agreed to come to Atlanta, which I mistakenly thought would be warm that time of year. It was not.

It is difficult now—in an age in which even James Michener's dramas are rolled out for an entire week on television, half of the scenes taking place with two people nude in a double bed, whether called *Space* or not (space without grace)—to realize what a furor the original *Baby Doll* caused when it first appeared in 1956.

In front-page headlines, the Associated Press reported that "Francis Cardinal Spellman, making one of his rare appearances in the pulpit of St. Patrick's Cathedral, today denounced the Warner Bros. film *Baby Doll* as an 'immoral and corrupting influence.' " (One might ask why the Cardinal didn't spend more time in the pulpit.)

The Cardinal chose mellifluous phrases to condemn the comic film. He said, "The conscienceless, venal attitude of the sponsors of this picture constitute a definite corruptive moral influence. Since these degrading pictures stimulate immorality and crime they must be condemned and, therefore, in solicitude for the welfare of my country, I exhort Catholic people from patronizing this film under pain of sin."

116

(I've wondered since what kind of pain sin causes.)

The sin was painted a block long on Broadway. There was a billboard advertising the film in which Baby Doll, played by Carroll Baker, had eighty-foot limbs and ten-foot eyebrows. She was coddled in a giant crib, sucking sensuously on her thumb: the virgin of Times Square. The Cardinal—called "Miss Spellman" by those who mocked him—had been good for business. The "welfare" of the country was in good hands.

But that was long ago.

I went south to Atlanta for a casting session and press conference. My plane was delayed, and Tennessee refused to begin without me.

Tennessee was his usual, generous self. When he was asked why he had waited to bring *Tiger Tail* to the stage and why Atlanta, he said, "I have been waiting for the right director. I have found such a person in Harry Rasky." Fortunately, he then added, "I have chosen Atlanta because I've always had a fondness for Coca-Cola."

We cast about for a local Baby Doll. We became aware how the Atlanta lovelies had long ago lost their innocence, or seemed to have, judging by those who showed up. They all seemed to have a supermarket hardness. But we found the perfect person to play one of the four parts. Mary Nell Santacroce, a local Atlanta celebrity, was the perfect sweet, slightly insane, Aunt Rose Comfort.

Back in New York, we shopped around for the other leading characters. Billy Barnes suggested Tennessee and I go see a current film, *Looking for Mr. Goodbar*, and we might perhaps find one of the young leading actors to be suitable. I recall that, after a light dinner, we went to a monster-size Broadway cinema, mostly full of blacks with giant boxes of popcorn, and sat uncomfortably through the film, which both of us found to be distastefully violent. The audience kept shouting, "Right on." It put us right off.

What made the evening memorable was that we bumped into Elia Kazan outside with a friend. We began walking together. There had been a slight shower, and the sidewalks were gleaming with neon reflection—the neon pavement. The broad avenue was mostly deserted. We all walked in semisilence. As we moved north on Broadway, past the scenes where the giant poster had once announced the coming of *Baby Doll* and other treats, at a time when as many as three Williams hits were running simultaneously, I viewed these two grandmasters together. Little had to be said by these two tense tigers. Together they had worked a revolution in the theater. Together they had dominated an era of world culture. They were veterans of many a creative battle, fighting like alleycats but finding strength in the battle, licking wounds and springing back for more. Now Kazan had left to find his own writing voice, and they were both diminished, in a way, by his departure. There would never be such a team again. I kept thinking of the title of one of Tennessee's short works, *Talk to Me Like the Rain and Let Me Listen.*

Finally I asked "Gadg" if he had any suggestions for *Tiger Tail.* First he said that the project had his blessing. He had read the stage version and thought it played surprisingly well. He recommended that Tennessee and I drop by the local tryout of a musical called *The Best Little Whorehouse in Texas.* There might be a girl in it for us.

Kazan never lost his warmth for Tennessee, and some of it rubbed off on me. Not long ago he wrote me, "I very much appreciate your devotion to Tennessee and I suppose we have been through the same revolving doors."

The phrase "Talk to me like the rain and let me listen" played on in my mind all through this period. It had been twenty-five years since I had "discovered" Tennessee on Broadway that hypnotic night as a student watching *Streetcar.*

At the Actors Studio, Tennessee and I attended the workout of the musical *The Best Little Whorehouse in Texas,* which seemed to have real promise, but Tennessee left after the first act and said, "They all look fine to me, Harry. Whatever you decide."

I never really knew which of the two girls Kazan favored, but I was caught by what seemed like all-American sweetness in an actress called Elizabeth Kemp. She told me later she had actually been born in Key West. In those days a pretty girl could blow me away with the flick of a false eyelash.

We would have had all we wanted in Sissy Spacek, but she wouldn't come south. Baby Dolls do not grow on trees.

Skilled veteran character actor Tom Toner read for another role. I liked him, and we became friends during the course of the next month.

This left only the key role, the dramatic hero, to be cast. We tried for Hollywood names, but when they named their price it became impossible. A local Canadian actor of Italian heritage was suggested to me. He read for me back in Toronto. With some nervousness, I suggested him for the part. His name is Nick Mancuso.

So on Christmas Day of 1977, we all arrived in Atlanta. There was an uneasy beginning. It being Christmas, the only vehicle available to pick up Tennessee and me was a large pickup truck. I said nothing, but Tennessee was almost full of claws. A pickup truck! As the days went by, he would express to the management his angry feelings at being picked up in a pickup truck.

The rehearsals got off to a lumpy start. Nick insisted on trying out various dialects, which made me uneasy. He sounded at first like Chico Marx. I approached the problem of stage direction in the same way I would a documentary film. I wanted the material to dictate to me its own strength. I wanted the direction to follow naturally and not be imposed on it. This makes actors uncomfortable. But I think it is truer to the material.

The most important part of directing this play was to spend as much time as possible with Tennessee. He was both teacher and comrade. We had virtually every lunch and dinner together and swam each day at the Peachtree Plaza, where we were housed.

His gentle humor was always there, and there was never an angry word between us. I recall one day we crossed the road where there was a plaque announcing that at this very spot, Margaret Mitchell, author of *Gone with the Wind*, had been struck down by an automobile. "Better hold my hand, Harry, two southern writers deceased at the same spot would make for bad drama."

Tennessee said, "I'm always afraid of offending people. I'm cowardly. The people in the theater, whether they like you or hate you, do their best. So I don't want to put anyone down."

He was totally supportive of my freshman approach to the stage. When he felt the actors were not reacting, he would say, "Do it like Kazan. Go whisper direction to the individual, so he won't be tense." It was good advice.

I confided in him that this was a difficult role for me because I was carrying with me the burden of having once tried stage direction in England, with a blank verse play called *The Heretic* by the Australian novelist Morris West; it had ended in disaster. An uneasy

119

star and I had clashed, and I had left the play before it became a West End flop.

I felt strongly about *Tiger Tail* that I could bring masculine strength to it. I concentrated on the sexual tensions, the teasing sensuousness that underlay it all. The humor was there throughout. Pounding the subtle sexuality into Nick was enormously exhausting. It finally culminated in a powerful performance, but it seemed to drain me and the other performers, especially the girl, who seemed to wither as he gained strength.

I was feeling very strong professionally. While we were in rehearsal, *Homage to Chagall—The Colours of Love* had been nominated by several New York film critics as one of the ten best of the year, including the highly prestigious and thoughtful Judith Crist and Jeffrey Lyons. There was a special screening of my film work by the Alliance, including *Tennessee Williams' South*, that Tennessee attended, his fourth viewing of the work. He and the film received a standing ovation.

The night before the official opening of *Tiger Tail* was wild and woolly. As part of the theater's agreement with the community, previews were set aside for busloads from a local state mental hospital. This play, once condemned as "sinful," seemed as innocent as a Saturday-morning cartoon now. The mental patients howled with laughter, shouted back to the actors onstage, and gave me the feeling this was what it must have been like at Shakespeare's Globe Theater. Live, really live. And Tennessee really loved it.

Opening night was just as spirited. When the audience roared with laughter, Tennessee glowed with pleasure and said, "You see, Harry? And they say only Neil Simon knows how to make them laugh. Listen to them laugh."

The bravos surrounded us when the final curtain came down. They called for the author, and Tennessee quite kindly insisted I take the bow with him. The audience cheered. I could feel how much he had missed this kind of night of nights.

That night of solid jubilation of the opening was my gift to Tennessee, in a way. All the usual tensions, self-doubts, inner agonies seemed absent. He was at home with his audience, and they embraced the work and loved him. He was swimming, yes swimming, with the adulation. *The Atlanta Constitution* carried a front-page headline with his photograph: "It's a winner for Williams"; *The Atlanta Journal* ("Covers Dixie Like the Dew!") headlined its review of January 20, 1978, "Tennessee Williams Takes a Bow—'Tiger Tail' Superb at the Alliance."

Perhaps most important, United Press International sent a critic who spread the word across the country: "Playwright Tennessee Williams—who set theater audiences afire in the 1940s and 1950s, but later remarked that he slept through the 60s and 70s—'awoke' to a standing ovation last night at the world premiere of his newest play 'Tiger Tail.' The play, performed before a sell-out crowd at the Atlanta Alliance Theatre, was Williams' first in years—and an instant hit."

Stories appeared instantly in the important theater centers. *The Chicago Tribune* columnist said, " 'Tiger Tail' is such a big hit in Atlanta that nine Broadway producers have flown down to see it. (His friends say it has done wonders for the playwright's spirits. . . .)" The *Los Angeles Times* gave prominence to the story. And in New York, the then-king of gossip reporters, Earl Wilson, headlined his column, "Tennessee's coming back." He wrote:

> Tennessee Williams is looking toward another Broadway comeback now that his latest show has given Atlanta such excitement as it hasn't had since the opening of "Gone With The Wind," "Author, Author," they yelled.

If only . . .

If only we had been able to convince somebody to move the hit play intact to Broadway. There were many excuses: The theater wasn't quite there, a producing team was split. Some said the set was too large. Others said it needed a star. Some claimed that Tennessee was out of style, too dangerous, wild track.

I personally wrote to several major drama critics, the ones who claimed they admired him so, to come on down, come and see his work the way he liked it. No one arrived. But for a brief moment I had the feeling of what he must have felt so often in his days of magic, before fashion dismissed him and his outcry alerted so many people to their own laughter and lamentation.

So.

I headed farther south for a few days of rest in Florida, attending my own film at an opening by the Flying Fendelmans in their cinema in Coconut Grove. Everyone wanted to talk about Tennessee's resurrection. I was pleased to have been at his side for his brief, late moment in the theatrical sun.

He was so much like the Princess in *Sweet Bird of Youth* in those trying days. He was in flight, trying not to be lost or haunted.

Flight. It was a kind of last chance. I suppose I knew it, even then. Even then.

I personally pleaded with the men who operated the Shubert Theater in L.A. The indifference of the Broadway powers was more than I knew how to handle. Billy tried, but nothing happened. The play would not be moved.

And there soon arose a kind of bruising personal crisis between us. Before I had gone south to Atlanta, I had written to the other great playwright of our time, Arthur Miller, about making a film with him and about him for my ongoing commitment to the CBC. While there, he replied, "The proposal seems a good one."

If you were selecting the greatest American plays of all time, you might come up with a troika: *Streetcar*, of course, *Long Day's Journey Into Night*, and without question *Death of a Salesman*. Since I had made the film about Tennessee, it just seemed normal that I would go to the other "bookend" of great stage literature, Arthur Miller. It seemed normal to me.

But what I did not realize, and I suppose I was naïve, was how possessive Tennessee felt. Not jealous; but for him, I suppose, in thinking back, it seemed at least a temporary loss or even betrayal. When I told him, he grew silent. It was his silence of aloneness. Our bond was bruised, I think.

At that time, Arthur Miller had been reluctant to face too much probing, with good reason. After the death of his former wife Marilyn Monroe, he wanted a time of silence. It was his steady, wonderful present wife, Inge Moath, the superb photographer, who convinced him to participate after they had jointly viewed my Williams film. Of course, the Miller story is another book. I only need say here that Arthur Miller was an understanding, helpful subject, and when the experience was over he paid me an impressive and appreciated compliment. He wrote, "Apparently people have found something like hope, God save us, in what you put together, and I think that's a wonderful thing to give them any time, and hard to do when the subject is a writer, the gloomiest breed." (Not "gloomy"—complex.)

For Tennessee, there followed a period of great depression. Nothing seemed to be working. Our encounters grew scarcer. I would write to him about my own problems. I recall feeling enormously let down when my Chagall film was nominated for an Oscar but did not win, and on the long plane ride home, I searched for kindness in a letter to him.

He had moved into an extremely unsuitable apartment in Manhattan Plaza, on the banks of the Hudson. It was a building of penitentiarylike bleakness. I recall having to go through a turnstile coming and going when I visited with him. I asked if he had to check in and out with the authorities. He had always hated any kind of restriction and spent little time there. When we went to lunch, there was none of the spontaneous fun of the stuffed peppers and the Monkey Bar. No doorman to give me my usual "Mr. Williams' brother" greeting. A man needs a certain amount of decay and dirt around him to feel comfort. And his new dwelling place was too cementlike for that.

He offered advice when I needed it. I had been asked to attempt a full-length feature about "freaks." It had only been attempted once before: a film by that name had been made by the imaginative Todd Browning in the thirties and had been banned by the same Church that went after *Baby Doll*, and Browning never worked again as a director. Tennessee urged me to try it. He said "Harry, do it. Do it your way. And make the audience wonder if the true freaks are in the audience or on the screen." It was good advice, and even though the film was greatly successful at film festivals and with teachers and a major award winner in Hong Kong, no key U.S. theater would project it. But I valued his wisdom. It comforted me and gave me courage to face the true freaks of life—and believe me, they were not the ones in the film.

I like what my favorite philosopher said: "I am convinced that the only people worthy of consideration in this world are the unusual ones. For the common folk are like the leaves of a tree and live and die unnoticed." That was said by the Scarecrow in *The Wizard of Oz*.

Tennessee so understood that. He wrote, "The biologists will tell you that progress is the result of mutations. Mutations are another word for freaks. For God's sake let's have a little more freakish behaviour—not less. Maybe 99 per cent of the freaks will be just freaks, ludicrous and pathetic and getting nowhere but into trouble. Eliminate them, however—bully them into conformity—and nobody in America will ever be really young any more and we'll be left standing in the dead center of nowhere."

He taught me this.

We should have learned this.

But in our way we all abandoned him.

My own contacts diminished.

There was then the evening of what I call "the great peacemaking." Christopher Isherwood had a new play opening on Broadway, *A Meeting By the River*, starring my dear friend Sam Jaffe, who had become honorary grandfather to my children. Tennessee and I both attended, but separately. I found him friendly but a little distant.

At the postcurtain party, I introduced him to Sam and his lovely wife, Bettye, both of whom had admired Tennessee so much. I had an opportunity to talk to Isherwood, whom I had not seen since the Hollywood screening of my film. It was an opportunity to explain to him how it was that he and I had happened to be uneasy collaborators on a TV film of many years ago called *The Legend of Silent Night*. I found him courteous and understanding. It was a night for a meeting of many.

I sat down beside a small woman who had a face like a friendly terrier. I was introduced to Audrey Wood, the legendary agent, whom I was now meeting for the first time. She told me she had seen my film on TV and admired it. She still seemed shattered from the parting with Tennessee that had happened so long ago. I was able to offer some consolation. I told her that in a conversation with me, Tennessee had actually wept real tears of regret about their mutually destructive parting. She thanked me several times for sharing that information that night.

She said, "I'm so pleased to know he really still cares!"

As for the play, as Sam Jaffe said with his playful humor—and he was so brilliant, as he always was, in his part—"The play did not last as long as the opening night party."

I would attend one more opening night on Broadway. He would attend one more opening night of a play by himself.

The gods seemed to have checked out into some distant motel, out of reach, out of town.

New York, March 26, Tennessee's birthday, 1980. There was a transit strike and a blizzard. All came to pass at the height and blight of the opening of *Clothes for a Summer Hotel*. It was directed by José Quintero. As a young man Quintero had worked wonders onstage. Now it was all nostalgia. The play about Zelda and madness was a mess.

Just prior to curtain, I spotted Tennessee with a friend sitting in a prominent, visible box overlooking the stage of the Cort Theater. He looked quite regal, out of another time, almost. With his beard newly regrown, I thought in that setting he looked a little like Lincoln. I made my way to the box, where I was suddenly a little caught for words, and I wished him a happy birthday. I added, "You're looking very fit tonight, Mr. President."

He seemed puzzled at my comment. He laughed uncomfortably, and responded, "Why, you too, are looking well, Harry."

I returned to my seat. The curtain rose. I could tell instantly, dancers dancing a last dance, an overused ritual, that the *Clothes* would not wear. I breathed a heavy sad sigh for him.

At intermission I went out for a badly needed drink, alone, feeling pain for the playwright. As I pushed back through the crowded lobby, Tennessee worked his way from the other side, came up to see me, and said, "Harry, hah. I sat through the whole first act wondering what you meant when you said, 'You're looking very fit tonight, Mr. President.' You're obviously expecting one of the actors to shoot me—like Lincoln."

"Or a critic," I joked.

He laughed as loud as I've ever heard him. He laughed across the crowded lobby, and then the curtain went up for a sad final act, and much later came clanging down.

The summer hotel would never see a real spring.

José Quintero had gone through his own kind of personal hell.

This was to be his last gasp as well. It was too late for him, too. He was to say of Tennessee: "Whenever I despaired of my own work, I thought of his courage in the face of so much pain, and I went back to work. I worked with Tennessee, this genius, and I saw the pain of creation and I saw the fleetingness of success. That's why he's so close to my soul."

That's why he was so close to the soul of every creative person. And who will comfort us now?

That night I had wanted to ask Tennessee a favor. But I knew it was not the time or place.

I had been writing a book, the story of my own life and work, called *Nobody Swings on Sunday*. I knew it was early to attempt such a work, but when is the right time? A Canadian publisher, Collier MacMillan, was anxious to publish it. In it, there is a chapter called "My Brother Tennessee," a sweet remembrance of our time together. I wanted very much for him to write a brief preface. It was the only request I was ever to make of him.

I decided to write him soon after the ill-timed opening. Having no faith in his ability to tend to ordinary matters, I even typed an envelope on CBC stationery with my return address.

I thought perhaps he must have been very angry at me, because months went by and no answer arrived. The book was published without a preface.

Then one morning, an entire year later, this letter arrived, full of the old fun and detail of our friendship.

Dear Harry,

I know you'd prefer a quick reply on a scratch pad than one on typing paper which I've just run out of.

The book is a beautiful work. Of course, I've so far read only the part about me. It is so flattering that I fear it may be thought I wrote the introduction for that reason only.

Of course, I will undertake it. Please edit it and let me see a photo-stat of the edited version.

Have just returned from one of those "speaking" junkets. Sometimes I think they are plotting to kill me. I no longer have a traveling companion—must handle a val-pac and heavy mss. case myself. *Four* plane flights there and back covering Knoxville and Lexington.

126

My cousin still recommends a local psychiatrist to me. Is that a subtle hint? She is taking care of Rose in her elegant new home in Key West. The brother (Stell's) is taking care of me. Both are gifted painters, especially Jim—and wildly eccentric. In other words, this is my scene. Have completed 2 new plays and a film script.

Eat only one meal a day due to digestive trouble— called "Pancreaitis"—must take 3 big "horse-pills" before each meal to digest it.

> Ah, well.
> You'll hear from me soon.
> Love,
> Tom

Remember me fondly to Arlene.

What made this charming but bizarre letter unusual was that the envelope also carried two return addresses, one in New York and one in Key West.

It seemed like the perfect time to mend our somewhat fractured friendship.

I noted with some loving tenderness that he signed his letter to me "Tom." This was the first time in our decade together that he had ever referred to himself as "Tom." So I wrote to Tom Williams.

May 5, 1981
Thoughts on the Arrival of a letter from The World's Greatest Writer of Plays, 1 year after.
Dear Tom:
Your letter of May 15th, 1980 arrived yesterday.
It prompts all kinds of questions:
Was the letter lost for a year?
Were you lost for a year?
Was I lost for a year?
If the letter was lost, what made it found?
If you were lost, where were You?
If I was lost did I notice?
Are any of the facts in the letter still appropriate?
As it concludes with: "You'll hear from me soon." Is that then or now?

Are the brother and sister team still taking care of you and
Rose, or are you now taking care of them?

And the plays now written, have they been replaced by other
plays?

Even the return address is marked both NY and Key West—
which must mean you are in both places or neither. It seems
like the beginning of a play by Tennessee Williams or did the
letter I am looking at on yellow scratch pad not arrive. You
may fill in the blanks or just suppose it's a plot against all of
us.

Even a year late, it is a pleasure to hear from you, and hear
you are more or less well.

(which you may no longer be).

I was not well then, but am now.

My film on Freaks, now called "Being Different", (a title with
no sex appeal), is now concluded. It was painful to make and
almost burned me out. It is quite beautiful and perhaps the
most meaningful work I have done. It may also never see the
light of day. It is more powerful than I can tell you. The pain
came not from the beautiful creatures I filmed, but those
outside. One of the unexpected pleasures was that I also
wrote the lyrics of several songs in the film, especially one
called "The Song of the Human Heart", which I like very
much. But we will see. I continue to be active with a couple
of other films in the works including one with Teresa Stratas
who is an amazing character, in or out of fiction.

About the book, as you will have noticed this being a year
later, more or less, the Canadian edition is out and has sold
well. I am negotiating for U.S. publication and indeed an
introduction from you would help, if last year's offer is still
legal or even still available. Could you?

I am anxious to hear more about your latest works. Maybe
it's time I tried again to direct another of your works. I'd like
to try. I have pleasant memories of an excellent production in
Atlanta. It would be an emotional fraternal act to try.

I hope Rose continues well in the outside world, I am sure
she knows something we don't about handling life. Arlene
and the kids continue to thrive in this far-away clime. Our
son, Adam, will be having his 13th birthday, Bar Mitzvah, on
June 27th, it would be wonderful if his uncle Tennessee
happened to be up this way.

Meantime when I am next in New York, week after next, I
will try and find you, in the hope that you are not lost in
1980 somewhere.
With love as ever. . . .
Harry

I think he was lost. Not in a particular year, but in a general
fear. He did not respond. Someone sent me a clipping from "Tropic,"
a Sunday insert in *The Miami Herald*, of an uncomfortable interview.
In part he said, according to the paper:

I used to be kind, gentle. Now I hear terrible things and I don't
care. Oh, objectively I care, but I can't feel anything. Here's a
story. I was in California recently and a friend of mine had a
stroke. He is paralyzed on the right side and on the left side and
he has brain cancer. Someone asked me how he was doing and
I explained all this and the person said, "But otherwise, is he
all right?" I said, "What do you want? A coroner's report?" I
never used to react harshly, but I feel continually assaulted by
tragedy. I cannot go past the fact of the tragedy. I cannot comprehend these things emotionally. I can't understand my friend
who is sick in California and who loved life so much he is
willing to live it on any terms.
    Sometimes I dream about getting away from things, re-
covering myself from the continual shocks. People are dying all
around you and I feel almost anaesthetized, feel like a zombie.
I fear an induraton of the heart and the heart is, after all, part
of your instrument as a writer. If your heart fails you, you begin
to write cynically, harshly. I would like to get away to some
quiet place with some nice person and recover my goodness. I
cannot, for instance, feel anything about my mother. I dream
about her, but I can't feel anything. All my dreams concern
earlier parts of my life. The other night I dreamt my father told
me I could go on the road selling shoes. Back then that's what
I wanted to do: go on the road. We remain children in our
unconscious. I am happy my mother dreams there is a horse
in her living room. Her father would never let her ride a horse,
so it is a happy dream. I won't answer the phone on Key West.
Every time it rings I am sure it is somebody telling me my mother
is dead. I won't answer it myself.

Yes, but eventually the calls would come. The phonecalls, not unexpected, but certain, would come. The bell telephone was ringing away his past. Oliver Evans, the only male link with his youth and the spirit of discovery and respect, whom he sustained with constant checks to help keep some comfort in his dying years, died.

Oliver was gone, and then finally Edwina, the belle of the ball, tyrant of his emotions, she would go.

At the moment of his own confinement, he had cried out to her, "Why do women bring children into the world and then destroy them?" And there was no answer.

Her final going would be a final release of sorts. But the past was becoming unwound.

I think he never wrote or said anything more meaningful than when he observed, "Snatching the eternal out of the desperately fleeting is the great magic trick of human existence."

I would have a last fleeting time with him. Not long before the inevitable phone call before the eternal, I was in New York working on a film on the great opera singer Teresa Stratas. I had played the Williams film for her. She had felt it deeply and put him back in the present tense of my mind.

By chance, in New York I picked up the phone just before noon, our old usual time, and tried the Elysée Hotel, having no idea if he still stayed there or if he was even in the country. To my extreme pleasure, he was there. No, he could not make lunch. But could I stop by right now?

I went speeding down to the Elysée. There was the greeting by the friendly doorman, the old greeting. "Yes, Mr. Williams' brother. We haven't seen you in a while. Your brother's right inside."

At the Victorian Suite, a new young man, looking like an eighties version of Superman, opened the door. Tennessee rushed to greet me. He embraced me warmly. We sat on the couch. He would not let go of my hand. He kept holding on, holding, holding on.

"Harry, Harry. You're here. Here. Wonderful seeing you here. Yes. Wonderful."

There was to be a tribute soon at some theater—he didn't know who was giving it exactly, or when it was specifically, or which theater—but he wanted me to mark it down, to come with Arlene, to be sure to come. It had been a long time. He was tied up for lunch. Yes, but soon we would have lunch, and what a shame because it was Tuesday, and he knew how much I liked stuffed peppers.

"Yes."

Yes.

Yes, I suppose I knew, even then, that I would never see him again. Something about the eyes. ("The eyes are the last to go out.") I said good-bye, still clinging. He still held my hand.

I sent a last letter. I have a copy of it here. The last line reads, "At any rate, my dear beloved pal, we are here and if you need us just cry out . . . truly. . . ."

There was to be no reply.

He had written in *Small Craft Warnings* that he hoped he would not wake himself when he died.

The question is, could he wake us?

Once more the phone rang. Once more the phone would carry the call for the passing of time, the passing of greatness. He had choked to death.

There is a symmetry to all things: Teresa Stratas called my home in Toronto to weep with us. She had heard the news flash in New York and called to say she was sorry and knew what I must be feeling and that it was my film that had made her break her own silence to reveal her heart. Others called my home like those wanting to sit shibah in the Yiddish tradition, wanting to express their own grief, to make a contact, to weep.

I was not there. Strangely, I was out in Tucson, Arizona, at a place called the Canyon Ranch Spa, where I go annually to detoxify myself, to remove the world from my bloodstream. There it is simple to say, "I am the mountain and the mountain is me" and to mean it.

So when Arlene called in tears and asked, "Have you heard?"

Heard what?

It was a Friday, February, 25, 1983. I had felt strange all that day.

Now I knew why.

I had been out of time during the dying in my life. My mother died when I was working as a news reporter in Kirkland Lake,

Ontario, in the Canadian north. My father went while I was thousands of miles from home—I was in South Africa working on a documentary for radio. And now I was in Arizona with the desert and the mountains. I was out of time and out of town.

When I heard of the manner of his going, a plastic cap stuck in his throat, I thought I heard that laugh that can never be forgotten. The large, totally unplastic man had choked on man's smallest invention. Blanche had feared being done in by a poisoned grape. Up in the balcony of heaven or wherever, he must have considered the stage quality of this bizarre departure. Exit by plastic. Ridiculous. If it had been written in one of his later plays, the critics would have ridiculed it as "warmed-over Williams."

We all need someone to talk to at the time of our lament. Sometimes it is the stranger who will show the kindness. I phoned the drama critic of *The Arizona Daily Star*, Jacqui Tully, and asked her if she wanted to come around for a talk. It was more a listening. To her credit, she came and I wept and laughed away my tensions.

By one of those coincidences of fate—are they really coincidences?—I had with me a videocassette of the film. I insisted on my own small wake with reluctant guests, who, I am sure, thought I was insane, lighting a candle in Arizona, and recollecting my time with Tennessee.

I considered cutting short my stay and rushing back for the burial until I was told by Billy Barnes that it would all be in St. Louis.

No. No.

"Dreaded St. Louis." "St. Pollution."

Tennessee, who dreaded confinement all his life—it was as real a scare as the bogey man is to a four-year-old—he would be confined at last, "cribbed, coffinned, confined," next to Edwina in a well-marked grave. No peace-giving burial at sea, as he had requested. I would not attend. I knew he did not want to be there. I would not be there to add my blessing to this final insult in a world that had insulted him so.

One thing became clear to me as I continued my walks among the eternal deserts and mountains parched by the Arizona sun: he was wrong about one thing at least. He had said, "As far as we

132

know, as far as there exists any kind of empiric evidence, there is no way to beat the game of being against non-being, in which non-being is the predestined victor on realistic levels."

Nonbeing in the flesh, yes. But no sooner was that gone, sunk into the depressing earth of St. Louis, than his spirit seemed to be everywhere. No day has gone by that I have not somehow heard his timeless lines and his out-there-forever laugh. We laugh together still.

The somber obituaries would have made him smile. The headline of the mighty *New York Times* would have been a special cause for comedy. It front-paged him, staring at us, possomlike, under the headline: "Tennessee Williams Is Dead Here at 71" (continued on page 10, column 1)." I know I heard him say, "Why, Harry, they sound as if they've just reviewed another one of my plays. Hah! 'Dead in New York.'"

And on page 10, in fact, the drama critic Frank Rich reviewed his life as if he had been called on to pass judgment, noting that "there are no second acts to American lives" (quoting Fitzgerald). Sadly, I think the intermission in his life had blinded the critics to the second act's richness. They didn't get it. That is why he was so offended, I think.

Near the end of his life he had incongruously gone up to Vancouver to be "writer in residence" at the University of British Columbia. The dean had seemed distressed to discover that he kept disappearing. Obviously, the dean had not listened. Tennessee was "writer in residence" wherever his head was. That was his residence. They didn't listen.

Only my friend Dan Sullivan, the *Los Angeles Times* theater critic, seemed to get it. He wrote of Williams' "sudden death" (no death was ever less sudden, dying every day as he did), "Writing was what he did, every morning of his life. Does a silk-worm stop spinning silk because they're buying polyester?"

He had to write—to make his silk, to comfort the world. He explained that over and over again. "I have made a covenant with myself to continue to write, since I have no choice, it is so deeply rooted as a way of existence."

Why writers write may be as varied as their styles. But all have common needs and desires.

André Malraux once said that a novel is the transformation of experience into destiny.

Balzac proclaimed that his narrative goal was to wrest words from silence, to wrest ideas from the night. (Tennessee himself proclaimed, "Mornings, I love them so much—their triumph over night.")

And Carlos Fuentes added, "This singular struggle of the novelist against silence and darkness becomes particularly acute in our own times, when so many words are noisy silence and so many klieg lights make us believe that night is day."

Albert Camus called writing an "honor" and said he entered "literature through worship."

Elie Wiesel, the ultimate survivor, asked and answered, "Why do I write? Perhaps in order not to go mad. Or, on the contrary, to touch the bottom of madness."

Tennessee frequently asked the question about his own sanity.

The point is, of course: Which of us would seem mad to God?

And the question is sometimes asked by those who do not fear to ask, in this era of the Holocaust, "not, is God dead—but has God himself gone mad?"

Perhaps Tennessee in his ultimate quest must be judged with that question in mind.

Judgment is not my game. Some have written what they call "critical biographies." What does that mean? You get A-minus in your life, 67 percent in Existence?

I am not sure that any judgment can be made about his personal existence. He has always been quite exact in explaining his eccentricities as being unexplainable.

About the human dimensions of his creations, he was vivid. He said, "I have always been more interested in creating a character that contains something crippled. I think nearly all of us have some kind of defect, anyway, and I suppose I have found it easier to identify with the characters who verge on hysteria, who were frightened of life, who were desperate to reach out to another person."

I think if his personal affairs could simply be stated as someone who wanted to *reach out* to another person, you would have what he was. Of course, there were the inner demands of the conflict of the flesh and the spirit. He was not a saint. He was the most full and the most frail—he was human.

I have learned that if you are a witness you must testify. It is an obligation. To look the other way and just say it was another time, another place, not my problem, is to condone half and warped truths. By this process history becomes a collection of lies and is self-perpetuating. I was there and must testify. To do less is to debase his legacy to us.

And then there are the books by those who say they are "his best friend." Is it something we do not understand about the ungay gay world, that a book will list endlessly detailed alleged sexual exploits in the same way as a plumber will describe toilet-bowl fittings with some pride? The kind of catalogue of "lovers" makes *The National Enquirer* seem as somber as *The Christian Science Monitor*. Is it that they don't know? Or is it that in that particular skin game the exploitation of a friend is considered fair game? Books that are more, as Truman Capote once said, "typewriting not writing" can only anger anyone who really admired and loved Tennessee.

It was that swampy world of the gay cannibal that eventually would do most to devour Tennessee in much the same way as he had written about it in his brilliant *Suddenly Last Summer*. I remember watching that film with him when it ran on the late show in Florida. He liked the acting in the film a great deal, but about the literal scene of cannibalism, he merely said, "Ridiculous—I don't think we taste that good." But by relying, as he did in those late years, on the "taste" of some of the hangers-on in the world of the night, he was partially destroyed.

Some may argue that he was preoccupied by sexual deviation because he wrote about it in some detail in *Memoirs*. "Why, that's because Doubleday kept in everything hot and eliminated the things that were humorous. It was once that thick but they cut it heavily. After all, they are in the book-selling business and had to think in terms of what was commercially viable. But the contraction of the book has shifted the emphasis, giving the impression that I'm kind of a sex maniac. I haven't got time to be a sex maniac, do I?"

I have heard this denied by his editors. But the same publishers did rush to push the purple prose of his "friend"!

Strangely enough, on several occasions when I visited him in Key West, I found him quietly playing bridge with the aged but beautiful silent-screen star Lila Lee, who was Jimmy Kirkwood's mother, in the gazebo, as quaintly as the group from *Arsenic and Old Lace*. Hardly exotica! He once laughed to me: "Who could possibly be fascinated by geriatric sex?"

I think he defied the gay spiders who tried to trap him in life as best he could, and it would be sinful for them to gain a victory after he is in his grave.

Too much has been made of Tennessee's unorthodox sex life. I will not attempt to explain it. I do know that all his life he felt the loss of physical warmth from his parents, and perhaps he was trying to find it in the thousands of searching nights. I don't know.

I recall in Atlanta, during the warm period of our daily meetings, that once he had dinner with my wife and children in a strange restaurant that had a trendy disc for a menu, and he focused on my children with more concern than any father I have known. He commented on Holly's changing moods (and signed an autograph for her, "To Holly Laura—many laurels") and expressed concern at the allergy pockets under Adam's eyes, resulting from his childhood asthma. It is our loss he did not parent a brood. If it is true, as one scholarly theorist says, that he was descended from Shakespeare by way of the dark lady of the sonnets, then consider the loss to generations to come. Once, fiery Anna Magnani said, "Tennessee is the only man I would marry immediately if he asked me because he is so full of emotion." Consider the possible by-product of that strong union!

I have a theory, probably faulty, that he could never find any lasting happiness in physical pleasure because in his strangely puritan mind he had defied the ultimate law of the universe, which states that there are negative and positive forces—male and female forces—that give each other completion, and he could never be complete. He was attempting to find in motion what was lost in space. I think he attempted to find in many what could never be found at all.

I don't know.

About his capacity to give I am certain.

I have always, being Jewish, been uneasy with the dogma of Christianity. But I would say this: in his way he was the ultimate Christian. He had that need to take on the suffering of the world and in that suffering try to save the world though his literature.

And even as I write this I can hear his voice saying, "Harry, yuh know. I think you go a little far."

Perhaps.

He said there was only "the past, the present, and the perhaps."

Perhaps.

Finally. His death meant that in the United States, PBS would once again carry the film *Tennessee Williams' South.*

The telecast would lead to a phone call from Dodd, Mead, which would suggest publishing the story of the film and the events leading up to his death.

Thus, this.

Obviously, by now, it must be clear that *Tennessee Williams' South* is a journey into the soul. Having taken that trip, now I can share it at last with you.

Having shared it now, at last, at last, perhaps I can take down those faded photographs. And begin again.

As sister Rose said, "Yes. Yes. Tom!"

Tennessee?

He said he had a wonderful and terrible life and that he wouldn't cry for himself. He asked if we would.

You are the audience. Your answer?

Perhaps at the end of Ecclesiastes we can find some solace. The last chapter says, "Vanity of vanities, saith the preacher, all is vanity. And moreover, because the preacher was wise, he still taught the people knowledge."

He did know us better than anyone else, didn't he? And he goes on talking to us, freely and intimately still.

Yes, yes, yuh know.

Hah!

A Last Letter to Tennessee. A possible Parable of the Perhaps.

January 8th, 1986.
Key West, Florida
Dear Tennessee:

So, I have come along with the blind in search of you.

The invitation had come for a Mrs. Lynn Kaufelt,
some months earlier to go south to "join authors, critics,
publishers, PLAYWRIGHTS, POETS AND SCHOLARS in Key

West for the Fourth Annual Key West Literary Seminar and
Festival." (No mention of friends or even friendly film-
makers.) The subject to be: Tennessee Williams. At first I
thought the request was impossible. There seemed to be no
funds to bring me down with the film. I had also a tight
schedule because of a pre-arranged screening of a new film
"Karsh: The Searching Eye" for a command performance of
the Canadian Governor General.

But then the first publicity brochure arrived and on the
envelope was the printed announcement: "Tennessee
Williams in Key West." How was that possible without the
film, the one and only film? And who would be representing
your interest?

I wrote an urgent letter back to the organizers saying
the film and I would arrive to speak for you. If there was
going to be a wake, I wanted to be there having a few laughs
with you.

So, today, I left the record-breaking freezing
temperature of Toronto to make the long journey. An Indian
limousine driver narrowly averted a young boy on his way to
school. It seemed to me that lines of fate were converging
like a Tennessee Williams play. Suppose I had not cried out
to the driver to swerve? How many lives would have
changed? My life? The boy's, of course. His family's. The
driver's. And incidentally the "authors', critics', publishers'
etc." awaiting your arrival, now on my film, in Key West.
But I cried out, and the boy went to school, and his family
would never know, and the driver continued with his life
unchanged, and soon I was flying First Class on a most
comfortable Eastern Airlines jet, toasting you and the days of
wine and roses ahead at 30,000 feet. I know how much you
always loved flying and I felt comfortable in that knowledge.
The skies were unusually cloudy and they continued all the
way to Miami, brooding above the beige and gold buildings
of Miami Beach.

I had begun to feel I was romanticising the weekend,
until *they* came along, as I waited patiently in the new
Eastern lounge. *They* were two blind men, clinging together
while one was pulled with authority by a seeing eye dog.
Two blind men, one seeing eye dog. One was fat. One was
thin. Tennessee, you would have stared with delighted

disbelief. Were these possibly the scholars, or more likely the critics, come to comment, to probe the residue of you? One looked about 23, dark-haired with a few days of stubbled growth. How do the blind shave? The other was perhaps a few years older, clean-shaven with a pink pear shape. They stared heavenward out of unblinking empty eyes as they boarded the Eastern jet to Key West.

They were joined by a stewardess, two blind men, one stewardess and one seeing eye dog. She asked, "Will you stay long in Key West?" And they answered, "Depends on the party?"

So, is there also a party for seeing eye dogs in Key West, or are they part of our group?

A gushing, trendy lady rushes up to me. She wears one of those parachute suits that has become fashionable among the female freedom fighters of the land. She reminds me she had once come to interview me about Tennessee Williams. She had been working on a PhD., unfinished now for ten years, obviously a work as complex as Schubert's most unfinished piece of music.

"I just had to come, to be with him," meaning you. Her eyes rolled upward.

Beside me sat a man with a large pocket computer. Figures blinked like flashing neon. I thought at first he was some high-flying accountant. I was advised that he was heading south on a sheer expedition of greed. He had come from Philadelphia to count his reward. He was an early investor in the search for sunken treasure of the Spanish galleon Nuestra Señora de Atoxha, and the diver Mel Fisher had hit the mother lode—$400 million in silver bars and coins, chests of gold coins, delicate jewelry and dazzling gems. My air companion was counting his winnings.

Behind, the blind men toasted each other with a laugh, "Well, here's looking at you. Hah!"

The vicarious gold digger looked glumly out of the window, stared at the gray-black clouds and said, "I'm sure we're not going anywhere."

The Eastern pilot, with a voice more high-pitched than the usual Gary Cooper-like sound came on the loud speaker cheerfully and announced, "Well, well, ladies and gentlemen. As you can see it's not too pleasant a day. We just might have to land at the naval base. But I thought we'd just go down and have a look around."

I suddenly became aware that the two blind men had not known until then that it was cloudy and that we were having trouble finding our way, and I wondered if the seeing eye dog could be helpful to the overly cheerful pilot who was merely going down to Key West to look around. And one blind man said to the other, "Why are you so nervous?"

The start of a wake without the corpse.

In twenty-three minutes we were on the ground, welcomed to Key West in two languages. As I walked off the plane, following the greedy man with the computer come to count his gold, I saw a blind man with a cane, obviously waiting for the two blind men with the one seeing eye dog. I felt the brotherly thing to do was to offer to point them out, as, obviously, he would not be able to spot his flying friends. He said that would not be necessary. I don't know what sensing organ they used, but when they arrived behind me, they all let out a simultaneous whoop and holler, a wild west sound, and I think the dog joined in with a glad-to-see-you bark and wag of his regal tail. Seeing eye dogs always seem to carry a special serious dignity with them. And the greeting blind man with the white cane asked his newly arrived blind friends, "Where do you guys want to go?"

And simultaneously, they shouted back, "We want to go to the bar."

The last I saw of them, they were following their seeing eye dog to the bar, three blind men in a row. And I have been asking myself since, how did that seeing eye dog know where the bar was?

I thought I heard you laughing, Tennessee. I thought I heard you laughing. What seeing eye dog would lead the critics and playwrights and poets and scholars in Key West.

Don't wait for an answer.

Although the search for gold in Key West real estate is obvious with condos being cemented into the coast line, the raucous old Key West still dominates. Duval Street still looks like part of the Universal Pictures tour. Sloppy Joe's still boasts that if Hemingway did not sleep there, he drank there, heavily at times. However, once it was a place for conversation. Now videos blare in sight and sound.

140

But those shrimp boats still glide out to sea, one of them perhaps awaiting your ashes even now. One of those blue-haired southern ladies who seems to know secrets known to few men, recognizes me and tells me a post-mortem tale. She tells me that she learned that Dakin has sold your mother's house in St. Louis for about $50,000, but that the buyers have found a couple of cardboard boxes in the basement that were reauctioned for $75,000 at Sotheby's. I don't know if it's true.

Did I hear you laugh?

I pass a sign that says "school for hypnotists."

From my balcony I watch the shrimp boats sailing out to sea. Perhaps it is time to sleep and prepare for the experts.

Day Two, Key West:

Today I saw for the first time the banner that crosses Duval Street, the main drag, announcing as if the circus had come to town that the town that shrugged you off is celebrating your return. You always said that they were merely awaiting the corpse. You are being welcomed home a hero, as long as you do not show up in the flesh.

The official opening event is announced for 7 p.m., Cocktail Welcome Reception, Havana Docks Bar, Pier House, Zero Duval Street. Why does everything now sound like the title of a Tennessee Williams play? I can see it now, "Zero Duval Street." Sounds like a detour off the Camino Real.

And I head from Zero Duval Street to introduce the first running of the film at Munroe County Library at 700 Fleming Street, but the roads are torn up as the constant construction of Key West continues. The crowd is mostly young, the paying guests of the weekend mostly having stayed behind at the Havana Docks Bar to be suitably welcomed, not allowing you to interfere with their pleasures.

I find I cannot speak. I had prepared a talk. But cannot talk. I had prepared a speech but cannot speak. I am so aware that the last time I was here was with you. And the lack of your presence is more strong than the present. Tears flow and I ask the audience to forgive if they can. I will try to return!

When the film is done, I am still undone. There is no

way I can share you with strangers this night. You look too deeply into my eyes, you stare too deeply into my soul.

I am restless around the Pier House square at night. I pass an open door, a young couple, a brother and sister from Miami, are listening in awe to the critic John Simon. He sits while the brother kneels at his feet, the sister, called "Childy" by the brother, is spread on the bed, enjoying the joy of her heavy-drinking brother, admiring the acid-tongued drama critic of trendy *New York* magazine. I am offered champagne and stop to listen in.

Simon seems smugly uncomfortable, although he seems to be happy with the adoration. I ask him if it is possible he did not understand your later works. He suggests that is impossible. I ask him generally if he is not troubled by the possible hurt a critic does to the writer, and in a way perhaps the critic adds to the writer's demise. Simon says that if a writer has something to say he will write it no matter what the critics say. And I remember the long, lingering pain *they* caused you.

I am out to find his weakness. He wears his certainty too openly not to be vulnerable.

The subject moves to the two biographies that were published the year before, part of the reason for this book. Simon says he will go up to his room and return with his review of the books as published in *The New Leader*, an obscure journal. Again the admirer from Miami passes out the champagne. It is obvious the cup of the evening runneth over for him. Simon returns. He sits stiffly on his throne. The Miami man now lays prone on the floor struggling to keep enjoying the fruits of the evening's entertainment. The sister, sprawled on the bed, nods a knowing nod. And I sit on the second bed as Simon sermonizes. The review is several pages long and is lyelike in its harshness. It not only criticizes the books themselves but a review by Gore Vidal that appeared in *The New York Review of Books*. It is articulate, yes, in that Simonizing way. But the words seem too large and the sentences too long and perhaps the sweep too great for what is essentially a small empty traget, or should be.

And now sweet revenge.

Around the third page of the oration, with Simon acting out all the parts, an actor on an empty stage, the adoring

groupie spread out on the rug, fighting off the mist of sleep
he can fight no longer. He flows into a deep champagne-
loaded sleep. Not only does he sleep but he snores, an angry
snore at that. Simon will not be stopped. He continues
through his voluble, contumelious destruction of the books.

The sister stumbles over the brother now floating in the
deep.

Simon takes no note. But his audience has left him long
ago. Deep sleep.

It is time to retire, and the evening of the weekend has
just begun. Tennessee, you picked a great one to miss.

Day 3, January 10, Key West.

They've gotten us up at 8:15 to board this bus marked
"special"—no exotic name like "Desire".

The ladies of the morning. With their multi-colored hair
the ladies board the bus as if on their way to a day outing to
the ruins of Rome or the streets of petrified Pompeii. You've
been a monument for less than two years, but now will be
studied as if Vesuvius had erupted on you in the year A.D.
79. We take our historic figures seriously. The morning is
cold and gray and even the space shuttle hadn't gotten off
the ground that morning. Large craft warning. We make a
second stop on Duval near the Christian Science Church. And
more ladies enter wearing "green tags" that are clearly
marked "observer." I half expect the bored driver to call out
"Next stop, Tennessee Williams' life . . . watch your step."

Is it possible that a life can be studied like dissecting a
frog in an anatomy class? But they have laid out $125 to
hear the experts dissect lines, analyze characters, find hidden
meanings.

Two hundred and fifty paid attendants have come to
read into you that which was never written. But then, a
seeing eye dog is not paid to think, only to lead the way.

And the bus passes a large sign: "Mary Immaculate Star
of the Sea." The signs are full of Tennessee Williams' titles
and the bus full of Tennessee Williams' characters.

A woman with a heavily scarred face, brutalized by
some accident of the past perhaps. I don't know. She sits
next to me to say how much she enjoyed your performance
in the film. She confesses, for it is a time of personal

143

confession, that once long ago, she checked into the Pier House Hotel for a week, just to see if perhaps you might walk by. Yes, this is true. I know that you found it hard to accept the passion of your following. The woman sighs a heavy sigh. "If I had seen Mr. Williams, I never would have upset him by talking to him." How sweetly do your birds fly?

Not far from the Church of God of Prophecy, the bus lurches to a sudden stop. A wild hung over driver had narrowly escaped a major crash. I am reminded of the scene of *The Night of the Iguana*, in the splendid production by John Huston, when the bus clanks across the Mexican back roads. And someone says it all reminds him of Marrakesh. Well, maybe.

Past the Howard Johnson's, Mister Donut, and the rinky-tink part of town.

We cross the Blue Star Memorial Highway.

And there near the pyramid of the town junk heap, where the southern buzzards circle languidly, we arrive at the Tennessee Williams' Theater. They've got you in concrete and glass, baby, you might say. But have they got you in life?

As the official day of dissection begins as I am reminded of the immortal couplet by another deceased poet, John Gay:

"Life is a jest and all things show it,
I thought so once and now I know it."

The official welcome is given by William Robertson, Book Editor of the *Miami Herald*. It is affable, as they say.

A serious set of professors sets out to pontificate profoundly on "The Playwright as Poet." John Malcolm Brinnin sounds off the alarm of the day, "If my understanding of this weekend is correct, we are here neither to judge nor memorialize him, but to engage him." And so on. But he is quick to say that your subjects were "greed, lust, yearning and self-deception . . . and to turn it into a popular entertainment . . . but we will still be asking ourselves where did it all come from?"

I have a hunch that by now you would have headed for the bar if there were one.

My mind wanders as the thoughts drone on. There is a sign posted in front of the dais which reads "FEH." I think perhaps it is a comment on the commentators, but I see the small print that reads Florida Endowment for the Humanities.

Humanity?

Professor Brinnin gets a laugh when he says that the public misunderstands what a poet is, "He is not someone who goes out of his way to see a rose garden." His comments are a mixed bag of criticism of plays such as *Camino Real* and high praise for the pauses in *Glass Menagerie* and a comment about "the mystery in the wings."

There follows Professor Kenneth Moore, chairman of the department of anthropology at Notre Dame, whose area of expertise seems to be the Jews of Spain and "a new translation of *The Revolt of the Masses* by Ortega y Gasset." So, what are we to make of that?

I decide that perhaps I can best commune with you by going for a midday swim, and missing the question-and-answer period. The woman cab driver stares at my name tags; yes, we all have name tags to remember who we are and not who we might become—and she asks bluntly, "Are you anybody famous?" I modestly say, "No."

She stares more closely and spells out the name . . . "H-A-R-V-E-Y Rasky" . . . and decides I'm not worth bothering with. "Never heard of you." She catches sight of a tow truck ahead and wildly begins honking her horn and shouting, "That's my boy friend . . . Love you baby!"

I see why you chose Key West to record your characters.

The afternoon session examines "The Personal Roots of Tennessee Williams." You might say, as you once did, they are giving you the MGM treatment. This is a mixed bag of a group. But I am impressed with both the scholarship and defense by the ladies. You have reached them. You have touched them and they are here to give no ground. Your troops are circling around you against the male kill. Virginia Spencer Carr is a towering figure whose voice is as southern as Coca-Cola. I note among her considerable past that she has had three fellowships to Yaddo Artists Colony and taught in Poland in 1980. Her grandfather was the first postmaster of Palm Beach County. His trek as "barefoot mailman extended from Palm Beach to Miami Beach." I had run into her the night of the opening of *Tiger Tail* in Atlanta, and she is very gentle in her approach, but stilletolike in her comments to Donald Spoto beside her who has just said, "There is much that is dangerous and much that is dreadful".

145

They are joined by soft-spoken Allean Hale, author of a book called *Petticoat Pioneer*, who has been following your southern trail. She reports on a church she saw in Mississippi that had a hand as a spire pointing heavenward. And this influenced you. She says that Japanese Noh plays also influenced you. This may be news to you. Listen:

"Whatever path would have led Williams to Noh, it had elements that suited his talents: the central monologue, the lyric language, the imagery, the fantasy, the theatrical effects. It resembled Greek theater, on which he had always drawn. It avoided his weakness, plot construction, since it was virtually plotless. Its minimal set and cast suited the way theater was moving. Its somberness suited his depressive mood. Noh presents some universalized human passion at a moment of crisis and suggests transcendence to a balanced existence; this aspect especially applied to Williams, who in the Sixties was wrestling with a crisis both artistic and emotional. Noh is centered on an idea, not a personality. Its characters are abstractions of that idea; its symbols, costumes, even its prescribed structure subtly reinforce it. To a westerner, watching a Noh play is like listening to a three-hour oratorio without knowing its score. Noh combines music, narrative. . . ." etc. I will not go on with this . . .

That same evening we returned to the theater, to have Kim Hunter do a cross-section of your theatrical ladies. It's been a long time since Stella. In a question and answer period, the producer Lester Persky asked a series of questions of Miss Hunter, who seemed to answer them before they were asked. I wonder if life really is that way: answers before questions.

I would like to have soared like a sweet bird of youth with the performance . . . but no such luck.

Later we sit around a plastic table back at the Pier House. Persky and Lance Wilson and Mel Gussow, the fine drama critic of the *Times*, who confesses he had written your obituary before you died. (But many critics were doing that.) And John Simon who, as a passerby commented, drank ice water to go with his blood temperature no doubt. Eventually a light tropical rain comes and Lance and I talk, and he confesses he could not remember what was said that night we all met in Key West so many years ago. And he says he

146

never really did understand you. How could he or any who have come to explain you? The focus is not there.

Halley's Comet is almost visible, but I think you were more elusive.

Perhaps the highlight of the weekend was when we were gathered for the final main luncheon. I sat next to Leoncia McGee, your black housekeeper, who has mysteriously grown a white-black stubble of beard. She now sits like you, hands folded in front of her, and has taken on so many of your mannerisms. That your comment of long ago that you always thought you were black seems to have solid meaning here. Tennessee in black.

I had never known that she had once worked for Mr. Hemingway and she confessed that she had never been to one of your plays. I can hear you saying, "Yah, Harry, and that's why we always got on so well, Hah. Hah."

Simon gave his long awaited, long address—he fell in love with long distance words—and it turned out to be a kind of comparison between you and Eugene O'Neill. It was a speech done with the aid of a thick dictionary, so ultra articulate that it seems to be in a foreign language. Lester Persky got up to say with some amusement, "I think Tennessee would have liked your report. First of all, it's the best review you ever gave him."

I ran the film, one more time, and this time, I felt you were there in the room. They filled all the seats and sat on the floor and listened . . .

And I wondered here back in Key West where we spent so much time about all of this: did they really know you, those who came to remember, and those who came to understand, and those who came to see or be seen?

At night in the Maxi-Taxi, the radio announces a stabbing—a guitar player has been stabbed . . . wild track . . . and the driver points to a man who wanders the street all night . . . walking up and down Duval Street . . . to mile zero and back to mile zero . . . like all of us in life . . .

And men in wheelchairs zip along the sidewalk, in a hurry without their legs. And I think I just caught sight of those blind men with the one seeing eye dog . . . and even the dog seems to be smiling, as the shrimp boats wait to go out to sea another day.

And I am sure I have heard again . . . and will always hear the eternal laugh of your lamentation.

Yours as always with love
Your soul brother
Harry